Swift Fundamentals:
The Language of iOS Development

Swift Fundamentals: The Language of iOS Development

Swift Fundamentals:
The Language of iOS Development

Mark Lassoff
with Tom Stachowitz

LearnToProgram, Inc.
Vernon, Connecticut

LearnToProgram.tv, Incorporated
27 Hartford Turnpike Suite 206
Vernon, CT06066
contact@learntoprogram.tv
(860) 840-7090

ISBN-13: 978-0-9904020-5-3
ISBN-10: 0990402053

Mark Lassoff, Publisher
Tom Stachowitz, Technical Writer
Kevin Hernandez, VP/ Production
Alison Downs, Copy Editor
Alexandria O'Brien, Book Layout

Dedication:

This book is dedicated to the LearnToProgram team. It's great to work with people who are friends as well as colleagues.

Courses Available from LearnToProgram, Inc.

3D Fundamentals with iOS
Advanced Javascript Development
AJAX Development
Android Development for Beginners
Become a Certified Web Developer (Level 1)
Become a Certified Web Developer (Level 2)
C++ for Beginners
C Programming for Beginners
Creating a PHP Login Script
Creating an MP3 Player with HTML5
CSS Development (with CSS3!)
Design for Coders
Game Development with Python
Game Development Fundamentals with Python
GitHub Fundamentals
HTML and CSS for Beginners (with HTML5)
HTML5 Mobile App Development
with PhoneGap
Introduction to Web Development
iOS Development Code Camp
iOS Development for Beginners Featuring iOS6/7
Java Programming for Beginners
Javascript for Beginners
Joomla for Beginners
jQuery for Beginners
Mobile Game Development with iOS
Node.js for Beginners
Objective C for Beginners
Photoshop for Coders
PHP & MySQL for Beginners
Programming for Absolute Beginners
Python for Beginners
Ruby on Rails for Beginners
SQL Database for Beginners
Swift Language Fundamentals
User Experience Design

Books from LearnToProgram, Inc.

Create Your Own MP3 Player with HTML5
CSS Development (with CSS3!)
HTML and CSS for Beginners
Javascript for Beginners
PHP and MySQL for Beginners
Programming for Absolute Beginners
Python for Beginners

TABLE OF CONTENTS

About the Author:

Mark Lassoff

Mark Lassoff's parents frequently claim that Mark was born to be a programmer. In the mid-eighties when the neighborhood kids were outside playing kickball and throwing snowballs, Mark was hard at work on his Commodore 64 writing games in the BASIC programming language. Computers and programming continued to be a strong interest in college where Mark majored in communication and computer science. Upon completing his college career, Mark worked in the software and web development departments at several large corporations.

In 2001, on a whim, while his contemporaries were conquering the dot com world, Mark accepted a position training programmers in a technical training center in Austin, Texas. It was there that he fell in love with teaching programming.

Teaching programming has been Mark's passion for the last 10 years. Today, Mark is a top technical trainer, traveling the country providing leading courses for software and web developers. Mark's training clients include the Department of Defense, Lockheed Martin, Discover Card Services, and Kaiser Permanente. In addition to traditional classroom training, Mark releases courses on the web, which have been taken by programming students all over the world.

He lives near Hartford, Connecticut where he is in the process of redecorating his condominium.

About the Technical Writer:

Tom Stachowitz

Tom Stachowitz was born in Florida but spent his childhood in northwestern Connecticut. He had always been interested in writing and technology but didn't begin programming until high school. Tom studied Journalism at the University of Indianapolis' overseas campus in Athens, Greece and, after living in England, Greece, New York, Arizona, Colorado, Washington DC, and Virginia and then serving in the Army, he returned to Connecticut to focus on writing and technology.

In his spare time Tom enjoys hiking, games, and spending time with his beautiful wife, Krista, and their two cats.

*Access the complete lab solutions for this book at:

https://learntoprogram.tv/book-lab-solutions

CHAPTER 1

GETTING STARTED

CHAPTER OBJECTIVES:

- You will be able to prepare your Mac to run Xcode and Swift.
- You will be able to get started with Xcode playgrounds.
- You will learn how to create and execute a simple program.
- You will understand how Xcode facilitates app development.
- You will create and run a simple iPhone app.

1.1 HELLO WORLD WITH SWIFT

Welcome to Swift Fundamentals: The Language of iOS Development! In this book you'll learn the basics of programming so that you can be prepared to create applications for Apple's iOS platform. This book is aimed at the complete beginner, so don't worry if you don't have any previous programming experience. We'll walk you through setting up your Mac to start developing and then we'll show you how to use Xcode and Swift to get started building your projects.

Swift is Apple's new programming language and it has been designed to be friendly, fun, and easy to use. It was built with a philosophy of ease and speed like a scripting language, but is built with the power and complexity of a compiled language. We'll show you how to use the Swift language fundamentals to get started on your programming journey!

The first thing that you need to do when you want to develop a Swift application is ensure that your computer is ready to use the development software. Xcode is the integrated development environment, abbreviated as **IDE**, that Apple provides for development of OS X and iOS software.

IDE

An IDE is a software application that provides a set of tools for programmers to use when they're developing software.

IDEs provide a range of features and utilities that make software development much easier and faster, and as you learn more about Swift development you'll begin to see how the features of an IDE are integral to the process.

Swift, Apple's new programming language introduced in 2014, is integrated into the Xcode IDE and allows for rapid development of iOS and OS X applications. In order to run Swift, you need to have OS X Mavericks, which is version 10.9.4. If you're not running that particular version of OS X then you'll need to update.

Setting up your Mac for Xcode is a simple process. The upgrade to OS X 10.9.4 is free to download in the App Store. Once the OS X upgrade is installed and set up, you're ready to begin setting up Xcode.

(If you're using a PC, you can use a Mac Virtual Machine, or rent a virtual Mac server for as little as $1 an hour from macincloud.com.)

Figure 1-1: It's easy to find your way to Xcode from the Apple developer site.

The newest version of Xcode is readily available at https://developer.apple.com in the "Download the latest development tools and SDKs" section. Click on the "Xcode" icon and you'll be brought to the main download page. Once there, be sure to choose Xcode with Swift, which will be Xcode 6. Currently, Xcode 6 is in beta.

Xcode 6 beta including Swift

Xcode 6 beta, including the new Swift programming language, is free for Registered Apple Developers. Sign in with your Apple ID to download. Xcode 6 beta runs on OS X Mavericks and OS X Yosemite Developer Preview.

⊕ Download Xcode 6 beta 6

🗋 Xcode 6 Release Notes

Figure 1-2: Once you've clicked on Xcode from the main page, you need to download "Xcode 6 beta including Swift."

When you click on the download link you'll be asked to log in as an Apple Developer. If you don't currently have a developer account, you'll need to create one. Creating an Apple Developer Account costs $100 and that $100 gives you the rights to publish any apps that you develop in the App Store. It's something that you'll need if you want to develop for iOS.

Once Xcode is installed and started, you'll be presented with three options. You can "Get started with a playground," "Create a new Xcode project," or "Check out an existing project." Right now we're going to use the Xcode playground, so go ahead and select that option.

The Xcode playground is a new feature in Xcode, and it allows you to simply and rapidly test your code without having to worry about compilation or complex options. Once you've selected the Xcode playground you'll have a few more field to fill, "Name" and "Platform." "Name" is the name of your new file and it can be whatever you like. In this case, we'll use "helloWorld." The "Platform" option is asking whether you intend to develop a program for iOS or for OS X. At the moment, to test the functionality of Swift and Xcode, it doesn't really matter which you choose. For the sake of the example, we'll select OS X.

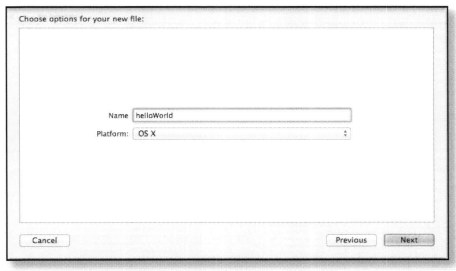

Figure 1-3: The options for creating a new Xcode playground.

After you've chosen a name and platform, you'll need to select a location to save the file you've just created. Once you've saved the file, you'll find yourself looking at a template that lists a couple of lines of code. Go ahead and erase the code in the template, but be sure to leave in the "import Cocoa" statement.

The majority of the screen real estate is going to be taken up the text editor. This is where you'll be entering in your code and doing a large part of your work. To the right of the text editor you'll see the gutter. The gutter is a useful feature that will give you a quick assessment of what your code is doing by displaying the current values of any variables that you're working with. In the template there is a declared variable called "str" that is given the value "Hello, playground." You can see this value displayed to the right, in the gutter.

```
var str = "Hello, playground"
```

Go ahead and add a variable by typing "var sum = 5 + 7" into the text editor.

```
var sum = 5 + 7
```

You'll see the result of that mathematical operation, "12", in the gutter. This is how the gutter helps you track what values are being assigned to your variables at any given time, often giving you a useful heads-up when there are any problems.

Figure 1-4: The Xcode gutter tracks the values of your variables as you develop.

This is a good point to discuss a very important concept in computer programming: **Variables**. Variables are used to store values that the program will need to work with later. A moment ago we created a variable that was called "str" and it was assigned the value, "Hello, playground."

Variables

Essentially, "str" represents the storage area where the value "Hello, playground" is stored. This value may change through the life of the program, however.

In order for us to create the variable we used a special keyword, "var." By using the keyword "var" before the variable name, we were instructing the computer to create a variable. We then gave the variable a name, "str," and *assigned* it a value with an **assignment operator**.

The assignment operator is the equals sign and it represents that we want to give the variable that we created and named "str" the value that follows. In our case, that value was "Hello, playground."

Assignment Operator

There are a number of types of variables that are used in the Swift programming language. The basic types of variables are Int, Float, Double, Character, String and Boolean.

Int, or **Integer**, is a variable type that is a whole number with no fractional number component. 12, 58, -522 are all examples of ints.

Integer

Floats and **Double**s are numbers that do have a fractional component. Pi is probably the most well known example, with its value of 3.14159... The difference between a Float and a Double is the size and precision of the number. A Float is a 32-bit number whereas a Double is a 64-bit number. As a 64-bit number, twice as much memory is allocated for a Double value than a Float. This results in more decimal places to the right of the decimal point and further precision.

Float

Double

A **Boolean** variable is a variable type that can only hold the values True and False.

Boolean

Character variables represent one single Unicode-compliant character, like a letter, number or punctuation mark.

Character

Finally, a **String** is a collection of characters that can represent full words, such as our "Hello, playground" variable from earlier.

String

Swift is able to examine variables created and determine what type of variable it should be. The value "Hello, playground" is a String and so when we created the variable "str" Swift declared it a String variable, with no input from us. We *can* also specify what type of variable we want to create in Swift. For example, do we want "42" to be an Int, or do we want it to be "42.0," which is a Float or Double? In those cases, we would tell Swift what we want.

Earlier we created a variable called "sum" and assigned it the value "5 + 7." This is a little different from the first assignment in that we're defining the variable as the result of an arithmetic operation. We are asking the computer to create the variable called "sum" and then assign it a value that is the result of the math problem that we put after the assignment operator. It's important to keep in mind that the right side of the assignment operator is evaluated first, and then the assignment is made.

Arithmetic operators are another very important part of programming, as they allow us to instruct our program to evaluate mathematical expressions. We used addition (+) above, but we could have just as easily used subtraction (-), multiplication (*), or division (/).

Now we're going to work on our first program. Erase everything in the text editor except for the line "import Cocoa." The reason that you're keeping that line is because "Cocoa" is a library that connects your Swift code to OS X and allows it to run on the chosen OS X platform. The first thing that we'll do is create a program that will output "Hello World." The "Hello World" program is the traditional first program that gets coded when learning a new language.

For demonstration purposes, in your text editor, begin typing "println()". While you type, notice that Xcode is offering context-sensitive assistance by suggesting code fragments that might be relevant based on what you are typing.

println()

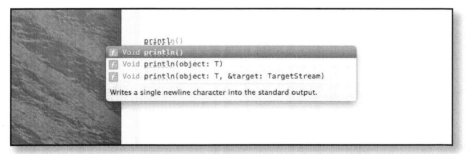

Figure 1-5: Xcode suggests relevant code fragments and provides information about them.

In this case, when you key in "printl" Xcode predicts that you might actually be typing "println()" so it suggests that for you and gives you information about the println() function. The small "f" to the left lets you know that println() is a function and the word "void" tells you that it does not return any information. At this point, if you press "enter" Xcode will automatically complete "println()" for you.

Functions are another basic programming concept and they will be covered in much more depth later. Briefly, though, a function is a self-contained collection of code that performs a specific task. In our println() example, you'll see that the function *returns void*. Void, in this context, means that we do not expect this function to produce a result for our program to use. Compare println(), which will print text to the console, with a function that we might name "addNumbers()" that adds numbers together. We would expect that the println() function will do what it is supposed to do—print a line of text—and then end. Our fictional addNumbers() function, though, would need to give us an answer in order for it to be useful. That answer is what it *returns*.

Functions

Now, inside the parenthesis you'll type in "Hello World" to tell println() what it is that you want it to print, and you're done.

Swift does not need a semicolon or line terminator to let it know when you've finished writing a statement.

```
println("Hello World")
```

In this example, by typing "Hello World" into the println() function you're telling the function what to print. If we're talking about our fictional addNumbers() function above, you might instead type something like:

```
addNumbers(1,2)
```

In this case, you would be providing the function with the values to add. The idea is the same: in both cases we're sending the function parameters. **Parameters** are values that a function uses to complete its task. If we didn't send "Hello World" to println() then println() would not be able to print anything. Similarly, if we didn't send "1,2" to addNumbers() then addNumbers() wouldn't know what to add.

Parameters

Once you finish typing your "Hello World" code, you will notice that in the gutter nothing has appeared. Earlier, the String "Hello playground" was visible, but your "Hello World" string is not. The reason for this is because println() is a function and the gutter displays the value of variables, but not the output of functions. If you had created a string with the value of "Hello World" then that would appear in the gutter. So how do we see the output of this function?

To do see the output of println() you'll have to run the program. To run the program in Xcode, you need to go to the "View" dropdown, choose "Assistant Editor" and then select "Show Assistant Editor." Once that's done, you'll have a new section visible in your IDE with the heading "Console Output." There, in the Console Output, is the result of your function, "Hello World." The Console Output shows you the results of your executing program.

Now return to the text editor and below your "Hello World" use the println() function to write "Welcome to Swift." You'll notice that as soon as you do this, you see the result appear in the Console Output of your Assistant Editor. It is also possible to write a mathematical expression in println(), such as "2 + 7", and see the evaluated result immediately.

```
println("Hello World")
println("Welcome to Swift")
println(2 + 7)
```

Figure 1-6: Xcode playground output displayed on the Console shows the results of your code.

Congratulations! You've just written your first program in Swift, using Xcode.

QUESTIONS FOR REVIEW

1. What does IDE stand for?
   a. Interactive Design Edition.
   b. Integrated Development Environment.
   c. Ironically Detached Existentialist.
   e. Internet Development Engineering.

2. What does the gutter allow us to do?
   a. Keep track of our program's output.
   b. Keep track of our variable values.
   c. Track code that we've deleted.
   d. Clean out incorrect code.

3. How do you define an Int variable in Swift?
   a. Declare the type and assign a value:
      int a = 5
   b. Declare the variable and type:
      var int a;
   c. Declare the variable and and assign a value:
      var a = 5
   d. Declare the variable and the type and assign a value:
      var int a = 5

4. Which of the following is NOT a Swift variable type?
   a. Int
   b. Boolean
   c. Long
   d. Double

1.2 Working in the Xcode Environment

The full Xcode IDE is much more than the playgrounds that we used in our first section. Xcode is a complete environment that allows us to create fully featured programs for iPhone, iPad and OS X.

Going back to the Xcode welcome screen, we're again presented with three options. This time, instead of selecting the playground, select the "Create a new Xcode Project" option. With the playground you only had, instead of the simple options to name the project and choose a platform but now, you will be exposed to the real power of Xcode.

On the next screen, you'll find yourself looking at a selection of templates to use for your new project. These templates provide you with a starting point for your app and create the basic files that you'll need. It is divided between iOS and OS X templates with subheadings for each. You don't need to know the details about each of these at the moment, but it's important to remember that Xcode provides these starting points for you when you go on to create more complicated apps and programs.

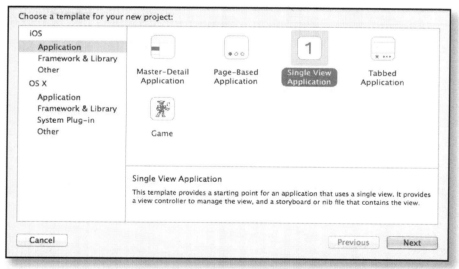

Figure 1-7: Templates available in Xcode allow you to quickly set up and get working on new projects.

For the moment, select the iOS Application tab and click on "Single View Application." This is the simplest application type and provides a great example framework for some of the advanced features of Xcode.

Swift Fundamentals: The Language of iOS Development

Once you've selected the template that you want to work with, you're going to be presented with another screen that has a number of text fields. These options identify your application and choose your application platform, like we did in the Xcode playground earlier.

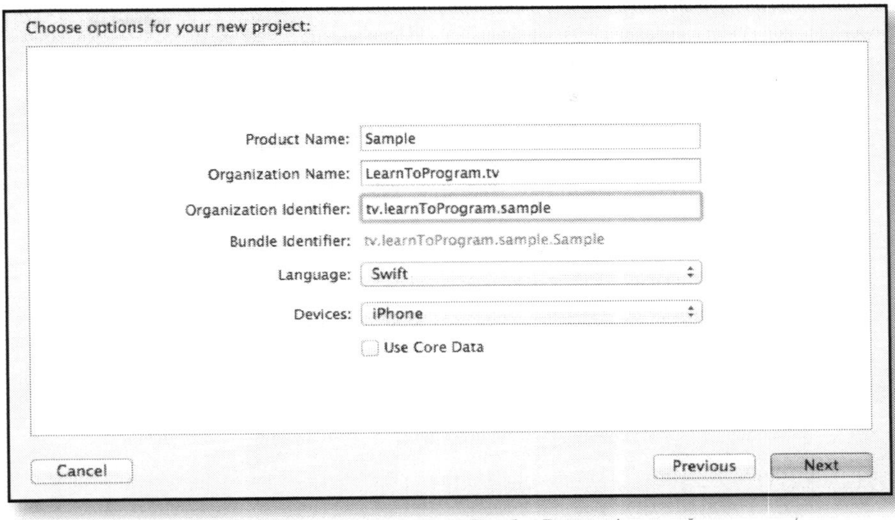

Figure 1-8: Setting up your first iPhone app in Xcode. Remember to choose a unique Organization Identifier.

The "Product Name" will be the name of your app, and the "Organization Name" is the name of your organization. This seems very easy so far, but what about the "Organization Identifier?" That is going to be the unique identifier for your application and it is custom to use a reverse URL. In the case of LearnToProgram.tv, the reverse URL would be tv.learnToProgram. We can then add a further identifier to the end, if we need to. In this case, we just went with "sample." This makes our Organization Identifier "tv.learnToProgram.sample." Below that you might notice that the "Bundle Identifier" takes the Organization Identifier that we just created and appends our Product Name to it. This allows us to use a single Organization Identifier and organize multiple products within it.

Xcode next asks you to choose a language. We're going to pick Swift because that's what we're trying to learn! Finally, you're asked what devices you want to target with the app. Although we already chose iOS, this allows us to specify if we want to make our app for iPhones, iPads, or both. For now, we'll just choose iPhone. Finally, we choose where we want to save our project. Much like in the playground earlier, we just need to pick a convenient location.

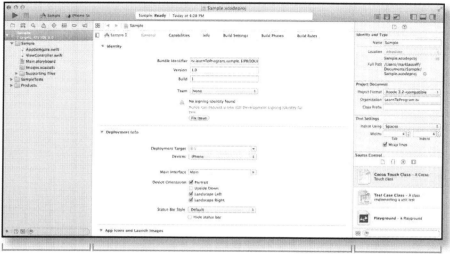

Figure 1-9: The Xcode main screen. On the left you can see the files in your project, in the center is your main workspace, and on the right are properties and toolboxes.

With all of that complete, we're now looking at the meat of the Xcode IDE. When the project initially loads you're looking at a project home page. Along the top of the main window you'll see a row of options that allow you to access various aspects of your project.

Figure 1-10: Xcode offers quick access to project options.

The "General" option shows basic information about your project, including things like the targeted device and its launch icons and images. Next to that is the "Capabilities" option, which allows access to modules that can be turned on or off to utilize certain functions like the Game Center or In-App Purchases. "Info" gives you general information about your project using key/value pairs. "Build Settings," "Build Phases," and "Build Rules" affect how the project is compiled to run and is something that you probably won't be worrying about for the time being.

Those options can be changed as you're developing your app. For example, once you get a better idea of how you want your app to be laid out, under the "General" tab you can choose the device orientations that are permitted by your app.

The directory tree to the left of the main window shows you the files that are used by your application. These were created based on the template choice that you made earlier and they represent the minimum that you'll need for your application to run.

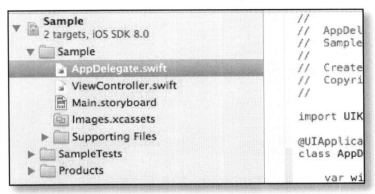

Figure 1-11: Files used by your project are readily available.

You probably recognize the .swift extension on two of the files, "AppDelegate.swift" and "ViewController.swift." If you open up the first file, which is the Application Delegate, you'll see some Swift code that is a little more complicated than "Hello World." Don't worry too much about this code right now, though. What the Application Delegate does is control how your app reacts as it moves through various states. Here's a good example from AppDelegate.swift:

```
func applicationDidEnterBackground(...)
```

This code is controlling what your app does when it is no longer the focus of a user's attention, for example, when the phone rings. The user sees the incoming call information come up and your application goes to the *background* and does what you describe in this function.

The other file is the View Controller, which describes the specific screen, or view, that the user is seeing. At the moment there are two functions there, both with the word "override" in front of them. That's something that you don't need to worry about right now, but it is important to note that these functions will help determine what happens to the view when the application loads. In fact, you can get an idea about the purpose of functions by reading the comments in the code.

When you're working on your program, it's important to think about **comments**. Comments in code are snippets of text that the compiler ignores. They exist only for the human behind the keyboard to read, and usually help explain what a particular piece of code does and, when dealing with more advanced programs, how various parts of the code interact with one another.

comments

As a project grows, it's easy to lose track of why you crafted certain pieces of code. Also, if someone else is working on a project with you (or you enlist someone to help) having well-commented code is invaluable in making it easy for them to understand what you intended. In Swift, commented code can appear on a single line after two backslashes, like so:

```
// This is a comment!
println("This is code!")
```

Or, it can appear on multiple lines between these two symbols, "/*" and "*/", like so:

```
println("This is code!")
/* This is
a multiline
Comment! */
```

```
import UIKit

class ViewController: UIViewController {

    override func viewDidLoad() {
        super.viewDidLoad()
        // Do any additional setup after loading the view, typically from a nib.
    }

    override func didReceiveMemoryWarning() {
        super.didReceiveMemoryWarning()
        // Dispose of any resources that can be recreated.
    }

}
```

Figure 1-12: Comments help describe what pieces of code do. In this case, automatically generated functions are briefly explained for you.

Don't worry if the comments don't clear things up for you when looking at the View Controller code; we're just trying to get a handle on how comments can be useful when you're programming.

The next file to check in the project is the "Main.storyboard" file. This is your application's Main Storyboard, which is where you can define the layout of visual elements in your app. While this can be done with code in the ViewController.swift file, Xcode provides you with a full-featured set of tools to make layout fast and simple. To demonstrate this, we'll create another "Hello World" app.

Figure 1-13: The Main Storyboard layout allows you to lay out and edit views in your app by dragging and dropping.

In the bottom of the right panel there is a collection of tiles with icons and text descriptions. This is your toolbox. In that box there is a row of icons across the top. Select the third icon from the left and then scroll down until you can see an option for a "Label." Now, all you need to do is to drag and drop the Label onto the Main Storyboard and follow the guides that appear to position it at the center of the screen. Once that's done, simply double-click the label and change the text to "Hello World" and you're finished.

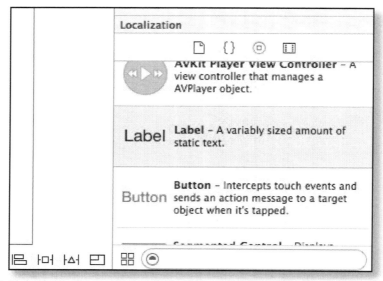

Figure 1-14: In this toolbox you'll find the Label for your "Hello World" application, along with a number of other useful elements.

Before we do more with your label, we'll talk about another important feature in Xcode: the ability to change which panes are visible. Above the far right panel are six icons that can help you organize your workspace. The default option, on the far left, utilizes the entirety of the main window for the file that you're working on. If you click on the second icon from the left, you'll display an assistant editor, which will let you view the graphical representation of the Main Storyboard as well as the code that supports it, side by side. Next to that, you'll find a view that allows you to display two code workspaces side by side.

Figure 1-15: Xcode allows you to modify the display and layout using these buttons in the upper right.

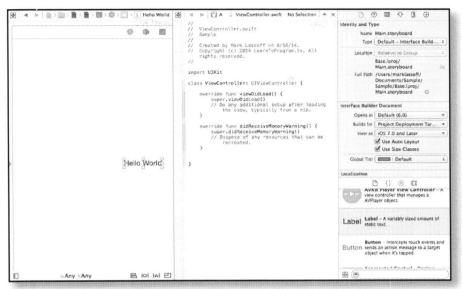

Figure 1-16: This is an example of a different Xcode layout. On the left is the Main Storyboard and next to it is the code that supports that view.

The three rightmost icons will let you determine which panels are visible: the left, bottom, and right. Within the right panel there are more identifiers that allow you to cycle through attributes and sets of controls.

If you select your "Hello World" label and then, in the right panel, select the third identifier from the right, you will see the properties of that label. From here, you can change the font style and size, making it larger and setting it to bold. All of these options allow you to do a substantial amount of configuration without writing code.

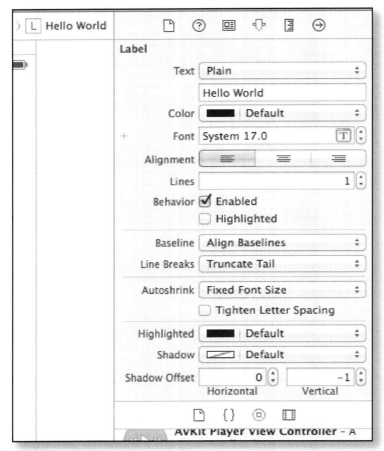

Figure 1-17: These are properties that can be edited directly in Xcode without ever having to assign them in code. You can quickly and easily modify layouts in your application.

Below the label properties, is the toolbox. In this toolbox there are a number of already defined controls and gestures in addition to the label that you utilized earlier. Adding a button to your app is as simple as selecting a button from the toolbox, dragging it onto your layout and changing the name. If you want to code for these items or instead generate layout elements with code, then you can bring up the View Controller and write your code directly.

Once you have created a simple layout with your "Hello World" you might be curious to see how it will actually look. There doesn't seem to be a console to output to, like the previous example...and besides, that wouldn't be particularly useful for an iPhone app. How often do you see a console on an iPhone app?

Xcode has a solution for this. Go to Product and select Run and you'll see that your program is building. After a moment, an iPhone simulator will appear and display the application that you've just created. This app doesn't do very much right now, so go ahead and stop it. Now what you're looking at is a still-functioning iPhone emulator. In this way, Xcode gives you the opportunity to create code for your iPhone and see how it will run without having to install it on a device.

QUESTIONS FOR REVIEW

1. What is a good use for comments in code?
   a. To meticulously detail everything your code does.
   b. To clearly and concisely document your code for future reference.
   c. Grocery lists.
   d. Nothing; your code should speak for itself.

2. What do Swift templates provide? Choose all that apply.
   a. A name for your project.
   b. The basic files that you need for a certain project type to work.
   c. A sample App Store page for you to modify.
   d. An outline for you to work within in order to speed up development.

3. Why is it standard to use a reverse URL when creating an Organization Identifier?
   a. Because URLs are pretty cool.
   b. In order to advertise your brand.
   c. So that your app shows up on Google.
   d. To help ensure that they're unique.

4. What does Xcode do when you run an iPhone app that you're developing?
   a. Launch an iPhone emulator to run your app.
   b. Display any output to the console.
   c. Send your app to the Apple App Store.
   d. Compile and run your app for OS X.

1) Ensure you have your development environment prepared with the latest version of Xcode. Open a new playground called SLA_Lab1. Go through the process of creating a playground as demonstrated earlier.

2) In the text editor erase any unnecessary code and leave the necessary import statement.

3) Create a multiline comment that lists your name, the date, and the name of the lab assignment (SLA_Lab1).

4) Using println() statements, output your name and address. These items should be the string arguments of the println() statement.

5) Output the result of the following expressions using the println() statement:

```
27 * 82
541.33 - 61.888
   999 / 540
```

6) Open the assistant editor and verify your results are correct when displayed in the console.

CHAPTER SUMMARY

In this chapter, we created a simple program that printed information to the console. We also took a brief tour of Xcode to get a taste of the features available. In the next chapter, we will go into more detail about the important fundamentals of programming that we discussed here, including variables, arithmetic operators, and a very useful feature known as typecasting.

CHAPTER 2

VARIABLES

CHAPTER OBJECTIVES:

- You will understand what variables are.
- You will be able to declare and assign variables.
- You will learn the difference between a variable and a constant.
- You will understand what the arithmetic operators are and how they work.
- You will learn how to use typecasting when working with variables.
- You will gain an understanding of string interpolation in Swift.

2.1 CREATING VARIABLES AND CONSTANTS

In this section, we're going to learn more about variables and we'll also be discussing constants. We'll use the Xcode playground to better understand how these two important concepts work, how to create them, and how—or, if—we can change them.

First, start up the Xcode playground like you did in the first chapter. This time, when you're picking the name of your program, call it "varsAndCons" because we're going to be looking into how variables and constants work. It's good to get into the habit of naming elements in a clear, easily understandable manner. We'll cover this more when we begin creating variables.

> **Tip**: We named the program varsAndCons. That particular pattern of capitalization is known as **camel casing**, and is commonly used in programming. With camel casing, the first letter of each word joined together in a name is capitalized to make the name easier to read and understand. For example, "number of objects" in camel case would look like this: "numberOfObjects."
>
> This technique is known as camel casing because the capital letters are said to represent the humps of a camel.

For now, from the dropdown, choose to develop an OS X application as seen in figure 2-1. As you did in chapter one, prepare the workspace by removing everything except for the "import Cocoa" statement. Now we're ready to begin working with variables.

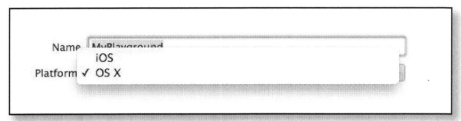

Figure 2-1: Choose to develop an OS X application.

In the first chapter, we touched on what variables are and how they work. A variable is a reference to an area in computer memory where a value we want to track is stored. When you initialize a variable, you are instructing the compiler to create a specific storage space in memory, of a specific size, and store a value there. The actual amount of memory reserved varies according to the type of the variable. We'll talk more about variable types soon.

Let's create a variable. In the playground, type the following:

```
var numOfStudents = 10
```

You should recognize this statement from chapter one. Here, we are instructing the computer to create a variable by using the keyword "var," then we're giving the variable a name, "numOfStudents." Next, we're using the assignment operator that we talked about before, "=", and finally we're telling it what value we want assigned to it, "10."

You might notice that we named our variable "numOfStudents." We did this because it's important to get into the habit of using readable, easy-to-understand names in our code. Here, it's clear that we want this variable to keep track of a number of students. We could have called it "numStu" and while we might have remembered what we were referring to, someone else looking at our code could have assumed that we were talking about the number of people named Stu, or something similar.

You also may have noticed that in the example code we started our variable name with a lowercase letter and then continued to use camel casing in the same manner as in the name of the program. While the the the Swift language doesn't require that we use certain casing, there is an accepted standard for naming elements that programmers tend to stick with. Variables will start with a lowercase letter but other constructs, like the classes we will learn about in chapter six, start with an upper case letter.

As programs become large and complicated, code is separated and organized in a variety of ways. Functions, which are covered extensively later in this book, are one example of this organization. When we're declaring variables, it's standard practice to begin their name with a lower case letter. Other elements that will be discussed later, such as Classes, begin with a capital letter instead.

Figure 2-2: A complete variable declaration.

The name "variable" also gives away something important about variables: they are variable. This means that we can change their value whenever we like. This is very useful, but there are circumstances when we would want to ensure that a variable is static and cannot be changed. In those cases, we use constants.

A **constant** is similar to a variable. However, a constant's value is consistent throughout the life of a program. In your playground, below your first variable declaration, type the following:

constant

```
let Pi = 3.1415
```

Notice the use of the keyword **let**, which creates a constant as opposed to a variable. The rest of the code should be familiar. We're naming our constant "Pi" and then we're using the assignment operator to set Pi to the value of "3.1415." The mathematical value of pi will never change, so why should it change in our program? This way, we can be certain that whenever we need to use pi, for example, in a function that determines the area of a circle, we know what value it will have.

Figure 2-3: "Pi" is declared as a constant and "numOfStudents" is declared as a variable.

To test all of what we've just learned, key in the following code and note what happens:

```
numOfStudents = 5
```

First, you should have seen a code completion pop up as you started typing in the name of your variable. Xcode knows that "numOfStudents" is a variable that you've declared and so it suggests it to you as you type. Next, you probably noticed that we didn't use the word "var" in this case. This is because we only use "var" when we're initially declaring our variable. Once the variable is created, we can just refer to it by its name. The rest of the code is familiar: an assignment operator followed by a value. In the gutter, you can see that your value for 'numOfStudents" changed from 10, as it was initially set, to 5. This isn't surprising because variables are, well...variable!

Figure 2-4: Code completion bubbles help you quickly access variables, constants and commonly used code.

Now, type in the following code:

```
Pi = 3.14
```

As you type the preceding example code, Xcode should have
displayed an error. To the left of your code there will be a large,
red "!" and the word "Pi" will be underlined in red. When you
click on the underlined code, a message will explain the error,
"cannot assign to 'let' value 'Pi.'" The error message is telling you that
you're trying to assign, or change, the value of a constant. Remember that
we used the keyword *let* when we created our constant "Pi."

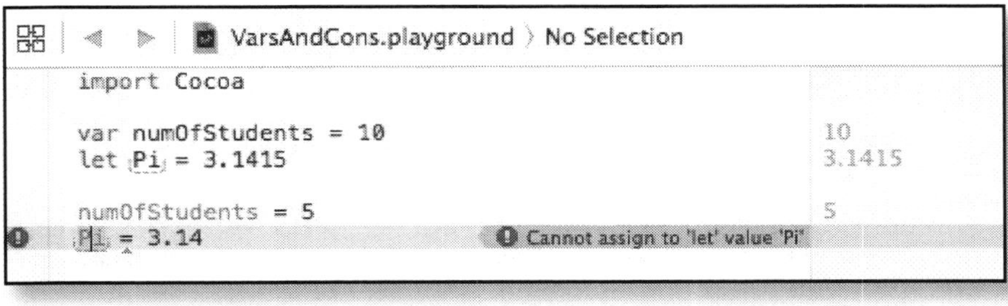

Figure 2-5: Xcode makes it clear when there is a problem and attempts to explain it. These
errors can be somewhat cryptic. In this case, the error appears because the value of a
constant is being reassigned.

Erase the line that gave us the error and instead reassign the value of
"numOfStudents" to 7. Now, your code should look like this:

```
var numOfStudents = 10
let Pi = 3.1415

numOfStudents = 5
numOfStudents = 7
```

When this program finishes running, "Pi" will have a value of 3.1415 and
"numOfStudents" will have a value of 7.

> **Tip**: You might have noticed that we declared our variables together before we started working with them. This is a good way to organize your code. Declare the variables that you're going to use first, give them readable names and, if necessary, type a comment that better explains what they're going to be used for. Then continue with your code.

In the first chapter we mentioned different types of variables like Floats, Ints (short for integer), and Strings. You probably remember that Swift can determine what type of variable is required when you declare it. In this case, "numOfStudents" is an Int and "Pi" is a Float. We also mentioned earlier that you can specify your variable type.

When Swift has inferred the variable type, the variable is said to be **implicitly typed**. Swift looks at the value assigned to the variable and assigns a type based on that value. If you're new to coding or haven't worked with a strongly typed language before, you may prefer implicit typing. Languages like PHP and Javascript are also implicitly typed.

implicitly typed

There is also the option of declaring an **explicitly typed** variable. In this case, we declare the type of variable in the code. This is useful because it gives us more control over development.

explicitly typed

Here is an example of an implicit declaration followed by an explicit declaration:

```
var age = 40
var numOfItems:Int = 77
```

The variable "age" is assigned the value 40 and Swift infers it to be an Int. "numOfItems," on the other hand, is declared explicitly as an integer variable. Enter the following code and observe what appears in the gutter:

```
numOfItems = 86.6
```

The value stored is 86, not 86.6. This is because we declared "numOfItems" as an Int type. When we attempt to set it to a floating point number by adding a decimal place, Swift ignores everything past the Int value. Note that the value wasn't rounded up to 87, rather, the incompatible part of the value was simply dropped and the variable was set at 86.

```
import Cocoa

var numOfStudents = 10              10
let Pi = 3.1415                     3.1415

numOfStudents = 5                   5
numOfStudents = 7                   7

var age = 40                        40
var numOfItems:Int = 77             77

numOfItems = 86.6                   86
```

Figure 2-6: When an Int variable is assigned a value with a decimal place, Swift will ignore everything that is incompatible with the Int type. In this case, 86.6 is converted to 86.

Nonnumeric variables can be set explicitly, as well. Recall the String variable type we introduced in chapter one. We can explicitly declare strings the same way we explicitly declared an Int, as shown in the following code:

```
var name:String = "Mark Lassoff"
```

In the example above, we instructed Swift that the variable "name" was to always be a string and then we assigned it a string value surrounded by quotes.

Explicit variable typing is similar to languages like C++ and Java in which all variables must be created with a type declared.

1. What is "Camel Case?"
   a. A naming convention that capitalizes all but the first letter of a word.
   b. A naming convention that capitalizes the first letter of each word.
   c. A method of transporting four-legged desert mammals.
   d. Slang for a cigarette holder.

2. How can variables be typed?
   a. Inferred or automatic.
   b. Dynamic or static.
   c. Implicit or explicit.
   d. Forced or suggested.

3. What can you NOT do to a constant?
   a. Declare it.
   b. Name it.
   c. Assign an initial value.
   d. Modify its value.

4. What should you consider when naming variables? (Choose all that apply.)
   a. How long the variable name is.
   b. How readable the variable name is.
   c. How relevant the variable name is.
   d. How clearly the name expresses what the variable is meant to represent.

2.2 UNDERSTANDING VARIABLE TYPES

Understanding why certain variables are used, when to use them, and what their limitations are very important parts of programming. To gain that understanding, we'll go through some exercises with Swift's variable types and explain more about their use.

First, open up a new Xcode playground and create a project called "VariableTypes." Prepare it by removing the template code then explicitly declare a constant Int called "anInt" and assign it a value.

```
let anInt:Int = 32
```

When you declare the variable, you probably noticed a code completion bubble pop up, suggesting some various types of Integers.

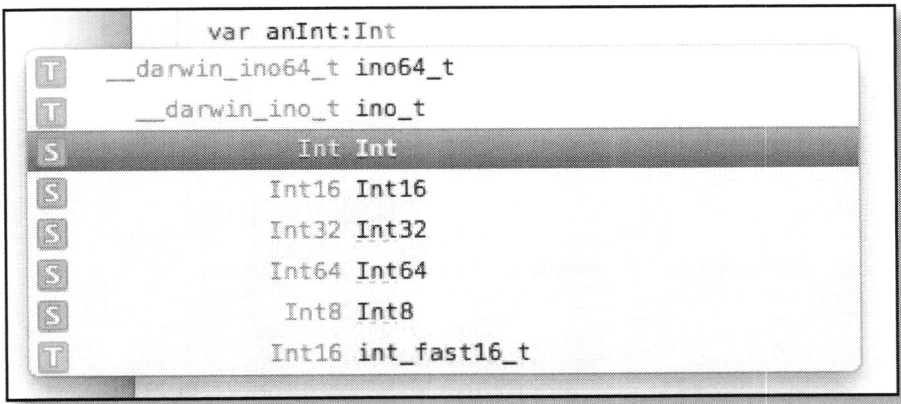

Figure 2-7: Swift code completion bubbles suggest the various types of integers when you explicitly declare the Int type.

When you create a variable, the operating system assigns a specific amount of memory to hold the information. When declaring your Int, it could be explicitly declared as an Int, an Int8, an Int16, an Int32, or an Int64. These different subtypes of the Int type determine how much memory is going to be reserved for your value. Int8 is an Int that's comprised of eight bits. (One bit represents a single memory address that can hold the values one or zero. A bit is the most basic component of data.) The maximum size of an Int8 is two to the power of eight, or 256. The other options are different exponents of two. Swift's default Int size is either 32 or 64, depending on the platform's native Int size.

Next, explicitly declare a constant Float called aFloat and assign it the value 10.05. When you explicitly declare it, you might notice that it is written as "aFloat:float_t." The "_t" is short for "type."

```
let aFloat:float_t = 10.05
```

If you're looking at the gutter (which you should be) you'll notice that although you've defined the Float as 10.05, the value is not exactly 10.05. Rather, it's a long, inaccurate number that is very nearly 10.05. This is a precision error that can occur with Floats, due to the amount of memory that Swift allocates to them. Change the value to 10.0.

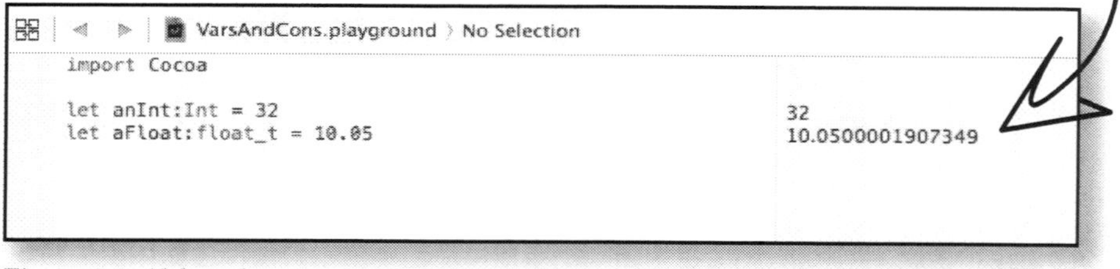

Figure 2-8: Although assigned the value of 10.05, the Float's lack of precision results in a different value in the gutter.

Explicitly declare a constant Double called aDouble to also hold the value 10.05. In this case, you'll see that there is no such precision error in the gutter. A Double is a more precise variable type than a Float, although in order to be more precise it does require more memory. Recall from chapter one that Floats are 32-bit numbers while Doubles are 64-bit numbers. Set your Double to any decimal value.

```
let aDouble:double_t = 5.0000008
```

Boolean type variables may only contain the values "true" or "false". We have not declared a Boolean variable yet but their declaration is exactly the same as every other type. Explicitly declare a constant Boolean called "aBoolean" and assign it the value "true" or "false." Your Boolean declaration should look something like the following:

```
let aBoolean:Bool = true
```

Finally, explicitly declare a constant string and set its value to any phrase you like. Remember that a string is defined by the text within quotes, so although you can use most punctuation in a string, if you attempt to use quotes inside of your string it will not work as you intend. Due to the nature of variable assignments, using quotes improperly will not always cause an error in Swift so you, as the programmer, need to be precise.

Your code should now look something like this, although the values that you chose may be different:

```
let anInt:Int = 32
let aFloat:float_t = 10.0
let aDouble:double_t = 5.0000008
let aBoolean:Bool = true
let aString:String = "A quick brown fox
jumped over the lazy dogs"
```

Now that we've explicitly declared constants, let's allow Swift to declare variable types for us. Declare a constant and assign it any integer value. Name the variable "anImplicitInteger." Next, on a new line, begin typing in the name of the constant you just created. You should see a code completion bubble pop up that suggests the constant you just created and you'll see, next to the name, that Swift inferred the type as Int.

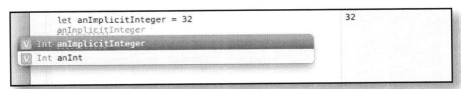

Figure 2-9: The code completion bubble shows that Swift assigned the type Int to "anImplicitInteger"

Now, complete the same process with a Float. Create a variable called "anImplicitFloat" and assign it a floating point value. Once done, check the type the same way you checked "anImplicitInteger" previously.

Did you notice a difference? Swift typed "anImplicitFloat" as a Double! The reason for this is that Swift cannot determine what precision you need with a floating point number. While a Float may be precise enough, there is nothing in the declaration that allows Swift to make this assumption, so it makes the safer choice and infers the type as Double.

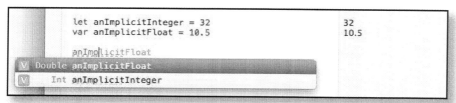

Figure 2-10: Swift will not type the variable "anImplicitFloat" as a Float because it cannot safely assume that you will only need Float precision, so it types it as a Double.

Finally, create a variable called "newVariable" and set its value as the sum of "anInt" and "aFloat." In case you don't remember how to do that, it's as follows:

```
var newVariable = anInt + aFloat
```

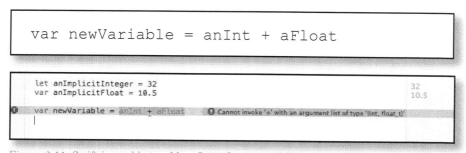

Figure 2-11: Swift is unable to add an Int value to a value, so it gives you an error.

Notice that Xcode gave you an error. This is because you cannot just add an Int and a Float together without a few additional steps. We'll go into how an operation involving multiple data types works later.

QUESTIONS FOR REVIEW

1. Which of the following are types of the Int variable type? (Choose all that apply.)
   a. Int8.
   b. Int16.
   c. Int2.
   d. Int 64.

2. A Float is more precise than a Double.
   a. True.
   b. False.

3 The answer to Question 2 above can only be either true or false. Which variable type would best be able to hold that value?
   a. Int.
   b. Float.
   c. Boolean.
   d. Double.

4. Why will Swift assign a Double instead of a Float when implicitly typing a variable?
   a. Swift is choosing the safer option because it does not know how precise you will need your variable to be.
   b. Floats are more difficult to store, so Swift chooses the easier option.
   c. The Swift developers just plain don't like Floats.
   d. Swift is designed for 64-bit systems so it always defaults to 64-bit variables.

2.3 ARITHMETIC OPERATORS

Once you've assigned a value to a variable, you need to be able to manipulate that value. This is where **arithmetic operators** come in. Arithmetic operators in Swift programming are exactly what you would expect: the symbols used to do basic math.

Start up a new Xcode playground session called "ArithmeticOperators" and prepare it as normal. We're going to go through the operations that are available in order to better understand how they're used.

First, declare a constant "a" and assign it the value 10. Then declare a variable "b" and assign it the value 5.

```
let a = 10
var b = 5
```

When you type "var b = 5" the computer understands that you want to create the variable "b" and then set it to whatever is on the other side of the assignment operator. Thinking about assignment like this makes it pretty clear that any computations on the right side of the assignment operator need to be complete before a value can be assigned to the variable on the left side of the assignment operator. This is exactly how it works: the right side of the assignment operator is evaluated first and then the resulting value is assigned to the variable.

Order of evaluation:

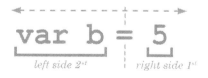

left side 2ⁿᵈ   *right side 1ˢᵗ*

The operators that can be used are the same operators that you're probably familiar with from school. There's addition (+), subtraction (-), multiplication (*), and division (/). There is one additional operator that you may not be familiar with called *modulus*. Modulus, expressed as "%," returns the remainder of the division of two numbers.

Arithmetic Operators

→ addition (+)
→ subtracton (-)
→ multiplication (*)
→ division (/)
→ modulus (%)

Before we begin coding, select the "View" dropdown menu and then "Assistant Editor" and finally "Show Assistant Editor." We'll be outputting to the console in this exercise instead of just using the gutter. Remember that the gutter only shows you the value of variables, not the actual output of your program. For that, we need to run the program and send the results somewhere. In our case, we will send the results to the Console Output window.

Figure 2-12: Make the Assistant Editor visible in order to view the Console Output window.

Let's begin with addition. Continuing from the preceding example variable declarations, declare a variable "c" and use the addition operator to assign "c" the value of the sum of variables "a" and "b." Your code should look like this:

```
var c = a + b
```

The gutter will show you the result, fifteen, but your console window will remain empty. In order to actually view the program output, you need to instruct the program to print the result, using the println() method that we discussed in chapter one:

```
println(c)
```

Now the console will also show the proper result and it's easy to verify that ten plus five is, indeed, fifteen.

The subtraction operator works the same way. Create an implicitly typed variable "d" and assign it the result of 1782 − 695.44 and then print the result to the console. Your code should look like this:

```
var d = 1782 - 695.44
```

Even though one of the values in your equation is an Int, the fact that the other value is a floating point number means that Swift will type the result in order to accommodate the most precise value. In this case, it will type the result as a Double. You can verify this by explicitly typing "d" as a Float and noticing that the result gives you the same rounding error we had when learning about Floats in section 2.2. This is due to a Float's lower precision. If you go ahead and type it as a Double, though, you'll have the correct answer.

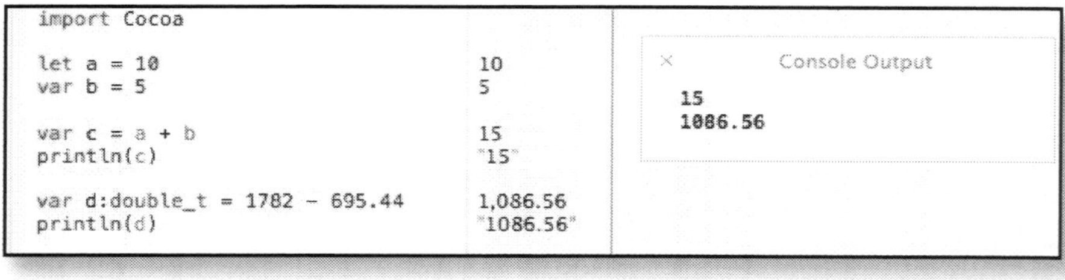

```
import Cocoa

let a = 10                                  10
var b = 5                                   5

var c = a + b                               15
println(c)                                  "15"

var d:double_t = 1782 - 695.44             1,086.56
println(d)                                  "1086.56"
```

	Console Output
15	
1086.56	

Figure 2-13: The Console Output window will show the results of your program as opposed to the gutter, which only tracks your variables.

Next, create variables named "e" and "f" and assign one of their values to the result of multiplication and the other to the result of division. You can either explicitly or implicitly type the variables, just make sure that the code is formatted properly. Also, remember to print the results to the console. You should end up with something like this:

```
var e:Int = 72 *109
println(e)

var f = 9087 / 16.55
println(f)
```

The final operator that we will discuss is the modulus operator. Modulus returns the remainder of two numbers after division. Enter the following code:

```
var g = 10 % 7
println(g)
```

You'll see that the result is three. Change the "10" in the equation to "14" and check the result. Now it's zero, because fourteen divided by seven leaves no remainder. In application code, modulus is often used to determine if a value is even or odd, since using a modulus of two will always return zero if a number is even and will always return one if a number is odd.

In addition to the traditional arithmetic operators that you are probably familiar with, there are the **increment** and **decrement** operators. The increment operator (++) adds one to the value of a variable, while the decrement operator (--) subtracts one from the value of a variable.

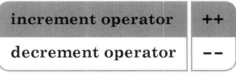

increment operator	++
decrement operator	--

With your console open, continue the example and key in the following:

```
b++
println(b)

++b
println(b)
```

Comparing the value in the gutter with the results in the console reveals something interesting. In the first scenario, "b" has the value of "5" in the gutter but "6" appears in the console. In the second scenario, they both have the value of "7." What's happening?

The difference is that when the increment operator appears before the variable it is considered to be a **prefix** operator, and when it appears after variable it is a **postfix** operator. A prefix operator will either increment or decrement the variable before its value is evaluated, whereas a postfix operator will act on the variable after its value has been evaluated. In the latter case, the resulting value will be used the next time the variable is referenced. Therefore, it is "6" when called by println(), but "5" when "b++" is evaluated.

prefix

postfix

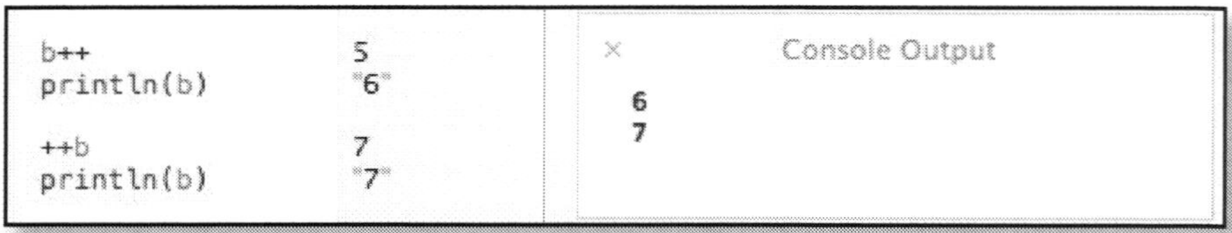

b++	5	×	Console Output	
println(b)	"6"		6	
			7	
++b	7			
println(b)	"7"			

Figure 2-14: Increments and decrements behave differently if they are *prefix* or *postfix* operators.

QUESTIONS FOR REVIEW

1. Which of the following is NOT an example of an arithmetic operator used in Swift?
   a. +
   b. %
   c. #
   d *

2. What is the purpose of the "%" operator?
   a. It returns what percentage the first value is of the second value.
   b. It returns the remainder from a division operation between the two values.
   c. It assigns the difference of the two values to the first value.
   d. It has no purpose.

3. What is a use of the modulus operator?
   a. Finding out if a number is even.
   b. Determining the difference between two numbers.
   c. Assigning a value to a variable.
   d. Removing a variable from memory.

4. The right side of an assignment operation is evaluated first.
   a. True.
   b. False.

2.4 TYPECASTING

So far, we've been learning about the different types of variables and how they are declared and assigned values. We've seen that once you define a variable's type, you may run into problems if you try to use it in the same expression as a variable of a different type. In this section we'll learn how to work with variables of different types in the same expression.

Typecasting is the way to convert from one type of variable to another. When we want to work with two variables of different types, we instruct Swift to typecast a variable, thereby making its value the type that we need.

Typecasting

I'm assuming that you're comfortable with getting the Xcode playground running now, so go ahead and start an instance. Once you're ready, create a variable called "value" and assign it the value of 145. If you don't explicitly declare this variable, Swift will declare it as an Int. You can verify that the variable is the correct type using the Xcode code completion bubble, as we learned in section 2.2. Now, attempt to set "value" to a floating point value, like so:

```
value = 149.99234
```

You'll see that Xcode doesn't display an error, but that the result of the evaluation of the variable, shown in the gutter, is 149. We discussed previously how Swift will drop everything that comes after the decimal point, but now that we've discussed variables in more depth, it's easier to understand why. When Swift declares an Int, it is reserving a certain amount of memory for a specific variable type. Space for floating point data is not included in this reserved memory, so Swift just ignores anything after a decimal place.

Create "secondValue," as an implicitly typed variable and assign it a floating point value of 99.22. When you check the status of this number, you can see that Swift declared it as a Double. We know that Doubles can be fractional numbers, but what happens when we assign a value that would be implicitly declared as an Int to a Double? Type the following into your playground:

```
secondValue = 85
```

If a variable were declared with the value of 85 it would be implicitly typed as an Int. In this case, though, we know that "secondValue" must be a Double. The gutter shows that assigning "85" to "secondValue" results in the value of "85.0." Once a variable is declared as a type it is permanently that type. To accommodate this, "85" is represented as the fractional number "85.0."

How are we able to work with different types if type declarations are permanent? Typecasting is the solution. When you typecast a variable, you're saying that you want to take the value of this variable and then use that value as if it were a specified type.

Going back to our "value" variable, it was most recently assigned the value of 149. Create a new variable that is implicitly typed called "preciseValue," but when you set its value, set it as follows:

```
var preciseValue = Double(value)
```

In this code, you're declaring the variable in the usual way by giving it a name, providing the assignment operator, and then indicating that you want it to have the value of "value," which we know is an Int, but that you want to typecast that value as a Double. The result is that the Int "149" is converted to the Double "149.0" in much the same way that "secondValue," above, was assigned the value of "85.0." You are then assigning to "preciseValue" the value of this new Double. The variable "value" still exists and has the Int value of 149. To confirm that the typecast worked correctly, add a fractional value to "preciseValue" like so:

```
preciseValue = preciseValue + 0.99234
```

This notation is a little different from what we've seen before, but remember that the right side of the assignment operator is evaluated before it is assigned, so in this case we want to set "preciseValue" to be the result of the value of "preciseValue" plus 0.99234. The result, as you can see in the gutter, is the Double value 149.99234.

Using typecasting we can utilize different types of variables together when we need to.

QUESTIONS FOR REVIEW

1. What does typecasting do?
   a. It changes a variable's type.
   b. It deletes a variable and makes a new variable with the same name of a different type.
   c. It uses the value of a variable but casts it as a specified type.
   d. It casts an actor in the same type of roles throughout their career.

2. A Double converted to an Int will be rounded appropriately.
   a. True.
   b. False.

3. Variable type declarations are permanent.
   a. True.
   b. False.

4. What is proper syntax for typecasting?
   a. floatValue = (Double)intValue
   b. floatValue = [Double]intValue
   c. floatValue = {Double}intValue
   d. floatValue = intValue as Float

2.5 STRING INTERPOLATION

A very useful feature in Swift is **string interpolation**. String interpolation allows you to easily use constants, variables, literals, and expressions in a string literal. The easiest way to explain string interpolation is to show you how it works.

string interpolation

Open up a playground and be sure that you can see the Console Output window by selecting the "View" dropdown menu and then choosing "Assistant Editor," and "Show Assistant Editor." Once you're ready, create a variable named "cookies" and assign it the value "5."

```
var cookies = 5
```

As you've learned, you've just implicitly declared a variable that Swift typed as an Int and then you've assigned the value of 5 to it. We now want to print to the console the number of cookies that we have. Here's what your code should look like, using what we currently know:

```
println(cookies)
```

When this code is run, the console will display "5." We know what the "5" refers to, but wouldn't it be useful to have some text that explains what the number means? We want our program to display how many cookies there are. To explain our variable's meaning using what we already know, we would enter the following:

```
println("There are ")
println(cookies)
println(" cookies.")
```

```
×                          Console Output
  There are
  5
  cookies
```

Figure 2-15: This code output gets our idea across, but it's not formatted the way we want.

You can see in figure 2-15 that this code does work, but it doesn't look right. There's a line break between the Strings and the variable that we don't want. One technique to fix this is called **string concatenation**. String concatenation is the combination of two string values using the concatenation operator. The concatenation operator is an operator overload of the arithmetic operator we have been using. We will explain operator overloads in chapter seven. If you have a string "firstName" and a string "lastName" you can *concatenate* them like so:

string concatenation

```
println(firstName + lastName)
```

The previous code would just make a single unbroken String, as seen in figure 2-16.

```
×                          Console Output
  MarkLassoff
```

Figure 2-16: The result of concatenation of two strings.

To achieve the desired String layout, you could enter the following:

```
println(firstName + " " + lastName)
```

The preceding code fragment concatenates the two strings with a blank space in between, returning the standard name format. Knowing this, and with your knowledge of typecasting, you could solve the cookie problem with the following piece of code:

```
println("There are " + String(cookies) + "
cookies")
```

Here you're typecasting your "cookies" variable into a String and then concatenating that String with the other Strings in println(). In the console, you can see that the previous code works, but it still seems like a lot of effort. That's where Swift's String interpolation comes in. Enter the following:

```
println("There are \(cookies) cookies.")
```

The console output should look like figure 2-17. What you've done here is instructed Swift to typecast the value of "cookies" into a String and place that String into the literal String that println() takes as its parameter.

```
×                    Console Output
There are  5 cookies.
```

Figure 2-17: The output of String interpolation.

This technique makes working with Strings much simpler. Create a constant string "name" and give it your name, and then use String interpolation to print it to the console, as shown in figure 2-18. You'll see that string interpolation works very well.

```
×                    Console Output
There are  5 cookies.
My name is Mark Lassoff
```

Figure 2-18: String interpolation works with constants.

We mentioned expressions as well. Create a println() command that takes the following as a parameter:

```
"My dog is \(7*3) years old in dog years."
```

Output this to the console and you'll see that the String interpolation handled the expression the same way an assignment operator would. It was evaluated and then the result was typecast as a String before it was concatenated into the println() parameter.

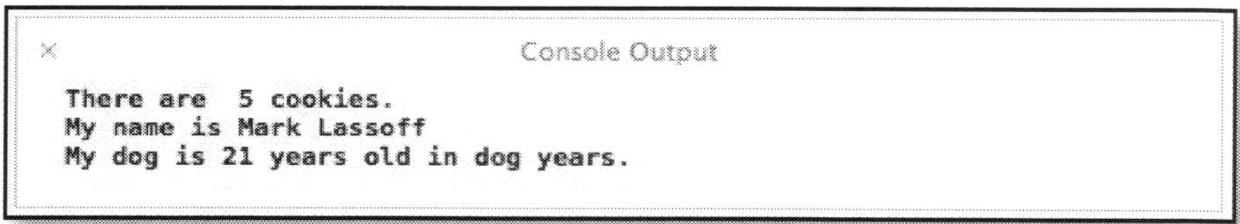

```
×                        Console Output
    There are  5 cookies.
    My name is Mark Lassoff
    My dog is 21 years old in dog years.
```

Figure 2-19: String interpolation also works with expressions.

Swift String interpolation is a quick and convenient way to work with Strings.

QUESTIONS FOR REVIEW

1. What is String interpolation?
   a. The act of determining what a String means.
   b. Including variables, constants, literals, or expressions in a String literal.
   c. Combining two strings using the addition operator.
   d. Converting other variable types to a String.

2. What is the proper method of String concatenation in Swift?
   a. stringA . stringB
   b. stringA + stringB
   c. stringA , stringB
   d. "stringA" "stringB"

3. String interpolation does not work with expressions.
   a. True
   b. False

4. Can typecasting be a part of string interpolation?
   a. Yes
   b. No

1) Open a new playground called SLA_Lab2. In the text editor, erase any unnecessary code and leave the necessary import statement.

2) Create a multiline comment that lists your name, the date, and the name of the lab assignment (SLA_Lab2).

3) Declare the following constants. (Don't forget that constants are declared with let while variables are declared with var.) Use explicit typing to create these constants. Use the type indicated below. As you create the constants, review the values displayed in the gutter.

Constant Name	Type	Value
score	int	67
rate	int	12.5
gpa	float_t	4
name	String	"Bill Johnson"
nameGPA	String	"Jane Smith \ (gpa)"
exactValue	double_t	27.84793392

Where the values displayed in the gutter differ from the value assigned, review the reasons why from the lesson.

4) Create the following two variables. You may use implicit typing to create them.

```
operand1 = 47.98
operand2 = 78.881
```

Output the result of performing addition, subtraction, multiplication and division using println(). Print out both the mathematical problem itself and the solution like this:

```
47.98 + 78.881 = 126.861
```

5) Open the assistant editor and review your results in the console. If you receive any errors or incorrect results, examine your code and rectify the errors.

CHAPTER SUMMARY

In this chapter we learned more about variables, including details about their types and how to explicitly or implicitly declare them. Working with variables is one of the most integral concepts in programming, so having a solid foundational understanding of them will make everything else we do in programming easier. We also learned about arithmetic operators and typecasting. As we'll soon see, arithmetic operators allow us to instruct our program what to do and when to do it. Finally, we learned about string interpolation and how to concatenate strings. All of these skills lay the essential groundwork for developing an understanding of programming.

In the next chapter, we'll look into how to determine what code is run using conditional statements and loops.

CHAPTER 3

CONTROL FLOW

CHAPTER OBJECTIVES:

- You will gain an understanding of the concept of control flow and why it is important to programming.
- You will be introduced to conditional statements and learn how to use them.
- You will utilize compound and complex conditionals.
- You will learn how and why to use a switch statement.
- You will learn about loops and use them to iterate through data.
- You will learn about different forms of loops: the while-loop, the for-loop and the for-in-loop.

3.1 IF STATEMENTS

In this chapter we're going to be discussing **control flow**. Control flow is the order that your program handles and evaluates the instructions that you give it by determining whether or not any given block of code should be executed. In its simplest form, control flow is what determines *if* your program should do something and, unsurprisingly, the simplest form of control flow is called the if-statement.

control flow

An **if-statement** is a construct that executes a code block if an expression is true. If the expression is false, then the code block does not execute. It's a simple concept that is fundamental to programming.

if-statement

To explore if-else statements, open up Xcode and start the playground. Select an iOS target instead of OS X.

Name	MyPlayground
Platform	✓ iOS
	OS X

Figure 3-1: Select iOS as your platform instead of OS X.

Name your program "ControlFlow" and set up the template as we have been doing. You'll notice that now you no longer have the "import Cocoa" line and that it's been replaced with "import UIKit." The reason the import statement is different is because you're developing with iOS as the target and UIKit is the library that will connect your program with iOS.

From now on, you're going to want to make sure that you have your Console Output window open from the Assistant Editor when we're working on examples. That's done by selecting "Show Assistant Editor" in the "Assistant Editor" submenu of the "View" menu.

The first thing you're going to do is create something that can be tested. We will declare a variable called "apples" and assign it the value "5." Next, we're going to create our if-statement. Enter the following code:

```
var apples = 5
if apples > 0
{
    // Do something if there are more than
zero apples
}
```

This code example is the basic form of the if-statement. The first line instructs the computer to test the value of "apples" to determine if the value is greater than zero using the greater than logical operator. The next line has an opening curly bracket to define the beginning of our code block for the if-statement. On the next line there is a simple comment that says "Do something if there are more than zero apples." We'll replace the comment with the actual code that will execute when the if-statement is true. The final line is the closing curly bracket that defines the end of the code block for the if-statement.

The above if-statement can be understood as saying "if there are apples, then do something." Therefore, if there are no apples the code block will not be executed.

Now that we know the structure of an if-statement let's use it to execute some code. Remove the comment and replace it with a println() that returns "There are some apples left." If you don't remember how the println() method works, it should look like the following:

```
println("There are some apples left")
```

Once you've entered the code correctly, your Console Output window should look like figure 3-2.

```
x                          Console Output
    There are some apples left
```

Figure 3-2: The output of your first if-statement.

Congratulations, you've coded your first if-statement! It doesn't do much now, so let's keep working at it. You might be wondering what would happen if there are zero apples instead of five. To test that, change the value of "apples" to zero. The console output will change from "There are some apples left" to an empty window because your if-statement only executes if the expression is true. To catch the false condition, we could use a second if-statement that tests for zero, but there's an easier and more logical way. Continue your statement like so:

```
if apples > 0
{
    println("There are some apples left")
} else
{
    println("There are no apples left")
}
```

Now examine the console window. It should display "There are no apples left." You can probably figure out how we got the result just by looking at the code. If there are more than zero apples, we want to execute a particular code block and if there are not more than zero apples, we want it to execute something *else*. That "else" statement has a clear meaning even if you've never been exposed to it before.

As you might have guessed, "else" in the above context tells the computer what to do when the if-statement is false. We call this an **if-else statement**.

if-else-statement

> **Tip:** There may be times when you don't strictly need an "else" statement, but often it will make sense logically.

Before we continue, let's take a moment to discuss **comparison operators**. We've already seen one comparison operator in the previous example, the greater than symbol. Comparison operators take two values, compare them, and then return either true or false. The result from comparison operation is what determines when an if-statement executes. Swift has six primary comparison operators.

Comparison Operators

→ greater than (>)
→ less than (<)
→ equal to (==)
→ not equal to (!=)
→ greater than or equal (>=)
→ less than or equal (<=)

We've already seen **greater than** (>). Greater than returns true if the value on the left is greater than the value on the right. **Less than** (<) returns true of the value on the left is less than the value on the right. We cannot test equality with the equals sign because that symbol is the assignment operator in Swift, so instead we use **equal to** (==). We can test if something is not equal with **not equal to** (!=). We can test if something is **greater than or equal to** (>=) or if something is **less than or equal to** (<=). All of these operators are shown here:

```
1 == 1  // True
1 == 2  // False

1 < 2   // True
2 <= 2  // True

2 > 1   // True
2 >= 2  // True

1 != 2  // True
1 != 1  // False
```

Continue the previous program and declare a variable named "testScore" that is assigned the value 100. Code an if-else statement that checks to see whether or not the value of "testScore" is 100. If it is, congratulate the test taker on achieving a perfect score. If it's not, inform the test taker that they received a less than perfect score. Your code should look something like the following:

```
var testScore = 100
if testScore == 100
{
    println("Perfect Score")
} else
{
    println("Less than perfect score")
}
```

Notice that even though we wanted to see if the score was less than 100, we didn't actually use the less than operator. In this example we're assuming that no one will make a mistake and enter a larger value than 100.

Now, just to ensure that we're on the right track, change the value of "testScore" to 99 and check the output. It should look like what you see in figure 3-3.

```
×                        Console Output

There are no apples left
Less than perfect score
```

Figure 3-3: The results of your first two if-else statements.

Testing your program as you're developing it is a vital way to stay on top of any errors in your code and to reinforce what you're learning. Another important way to make sure that you know what's going on is to walk yourself through the program. In our example above, we would see that the value of "testScore" is 99 and that the if-statement is checking to see if "testScore" is 100. The condition would evaluate to false and the if-statement's code block would not run. Instead, the else statement would run and the program would output "Less than perfect score."

Let's continue our example. Declare a variable called "gpa" and assign it the value "3.0." Check to see if "gpa" is less than or equal to 3.0. If it is, print to the console "You have less than a B average." If "gpa" is not less than or equal to 3.0, print the line "You have a B average or higher." Your complete code should look like the following example:

```
var gpa = 3.0
if gpa <= 3.0
{
    println("You have less than a B
average")
} else
{
    println("You have a B average or
higher")
}
```

The console output should be, "You have less than a B average." Looking at the result, it seems to be incorrect. A student who has a 3.0 GPA does have a B average. The program functions properly, but using less than or equal to didn't give us the correct result. The problem isn't in our code syntax, the problem is in how we designed our if-else statement. Change the less than or equal to symbol to the appropriate comparison operator so that the if-else statement returns "You have a B average or higher" if "gpa" is equal to the value 3.0.

```
var gpa = 3.0
if gpa < 3.0
{
    println("You have less than a B
average")
} else
{
    println("You have a B average or
higher")
}
```

Once the program is done, you can double-check your work by setting "gpa" higher than 3.0 and then lower than 3.0. The Console Output window should update appropriately. If you set your "gpa" to the value 2.995, for example, your console output for the entire program should match what you see here in figure 3-4.

```
 ×                          Console Output
    There are no apples left
    Less than perfect score
    You have less than a B average
```

Figure 3-4: This should be your console output after completing Section 3-1.

If-else statements are a major part of programming and in the next section we'll look at how we can use them in more complex ways.

QUESTIONS FOR REVIEW

1. What is the purpose of flow control?
   a. It determines what code is run at what time.
   b. It keeps track of your variable types.
   c. It ensures that your syntax is correct.
   d. It controls the file your program uses.

2. Which of the following is not a comparison operator?
   a. >
   b. <
   c. =
   d. >=

3. An else-statement runs whether or not the preceding if-statement ran.
   a. True.
   b. False.

4. How does an if statement know if it should run?
   a. It is named and called by the programmer.
   b. It runs once the program reaches it.
   c. It only runs if its statement evaluates to "true."
   d. It should never run, it's only there to help readability.

3.2 COMPLEX AND COMPOUND IF STATEMENTS

If-statements and if-else statements are useful for testing a single value, but what if we want to test multiple values at the same time? In certain situations you might only want an event to occur if multiple conditions are met. For example, a person can vote if they're above the legal voting age *and* if they're a citizen. Similarly, we might want an action to occur if any one of a number of conditions are met. A school might admit students based on their GPA *or* based on a test score.

There is a way to handle situations with multiple conditions in programming and it is through the use of **compound conditionals**. A compound conditional is a conditional that evaluates more than one expression in order to return true or false. In our first example, citizenship, the compound conditional would return true if both conditions evaluated to true, and in the second example, school admission, it would return true if either value evaluated to true.

> **Compound Conditionals**

Let's get coding to see how compound conditionals work in practice. Create a new playground called "ComplexConditionals."

Once you're up and running, create and assign a Boolean variable named "citizen" and an Int variable named age. Remember, with both variables you can either explicitly type your variable or allow Swift to implicitly type it. A Boolean will be set implicitly if the value is declared as "true" or "false." We'll set our values as follows:

```
var citizen = true
var age = 19
```

Next, create an if-statement that first checks to see if "citizen" is true and, if so, outputs "You are eligible to vote" to the console. You know that the code is evaluating the value of one variable, "citizen," and then using the comparison operator to determine the result of the condition. Your code should look like the following:

```
if citizen == true
{
    println("You are eligible to vote.")
}
```

A person has to be a citizen to be eligible to vote, but they also have to be 18 or older. Add the following to your if-statement, after the word "true":

```
&& age >= 18
```

Right now, your code and the output should look something like what we have in figure 3-5.

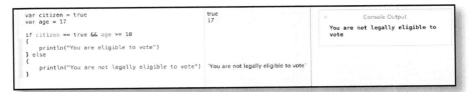

Figure 3-5 The result of your first compound conditional.

Those two symbols, called ampersands, are the "and" symbol in coding. What you've instructed Swift to do is to return true and run the if-statement code block when both the value of "citizen" is "true" and the value of "age" is greater than or equal to 18.

"and"

To verify the code you've just entered, add an else statement that prints out "You are not legally eligible to vote." Modify the values of "citizen" and "age" to verify that everything works as intended. You should see results that look like figures 3-6 and 3-7.

```
var citizen = true                                  true
var age = 17                                         17

if citizen == true && age >= 18
{
    println("You are eligible to vote")
} else
{
    println("You are not legally eligible to vote")   "You are not legally eligible to vote"
}
```

Console Output
You are not legally eligible to
vote

Figure 3-6: The if-statement is false if "age" is too low.

```
var citizen = false                          false
var age = 19                                 19

if citizen == true && age >= 18
{
    println("You are eligible to vote")
} else
{
    println("You are not legally eligible to vote")    "You are not legally eligible to vote"
}
```

	Console Output
×	You are not legally eligible to vote

Figure 3-7: The if-statement is also false if "citizen" is false.

The preceding example covers situations when we want to make sure both conditions are true. What about situations when we want to see if any one of multiple conditions are true? In that case, the compound conditional is going to use "||," which is the "or" symbol. The vertical bars are referred to as the "pipe" symbols.

"or"

Imagine a situation where a student is seeking admission to a school and in order to be accepted they need to either have a certain GPA *or* they need to have scored high enough on a particular test. Declare "gpa" and "testScore" variables and assign reasonable values to them. We've chosen to assign them as follows:

```
var gpa = 3.25
var testScore = 1500
```

Enter an appropriate if-statement, testing first to see if their GPA is higher than 3.0 and, if it is, printing "Student is admitted." It should look like the following:

```
if gpa > 3.0
{
println("Student is admitted")
}
```

After you've verified the code you've just entered, use the "or" symbol to add a second condition that tests to see if "testScore" is high enough for admission.

```
if gpa > 3.0 || testScore > 1600
{
    Println("Student is admitted")
}
```

In figure 3-8 you can see that we used the value 1600 in our conditional.

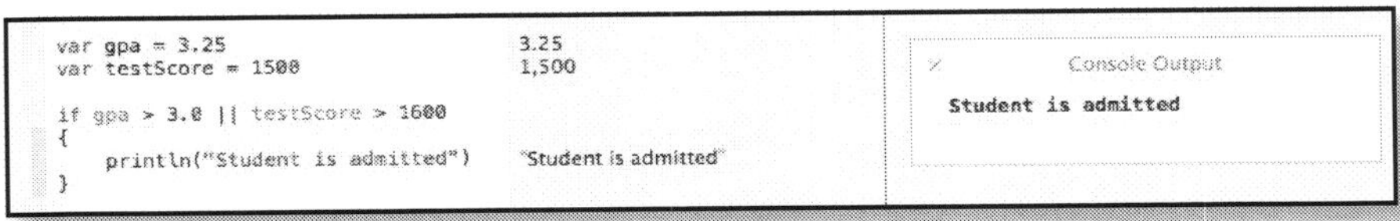

Figure 3-8: The result of a compound conditional using "or"

The example code is evaluating whether "gpa" is higher than 3.0, which is true, and then evaluating whether "testScore" is higher than 1500, which is false. The conditional returns true because it's an "or" statement and only one of the conditionals has to return "true" for the entire statement to be "true." In the case of our example, because "gpa" is greater than 3.0, the if-statement is true.

Create your else statement so that your if-else statement will return "Student is not admitted" when both conditions are false. Verify your code by modifying the values of "gpa" and "testScore."

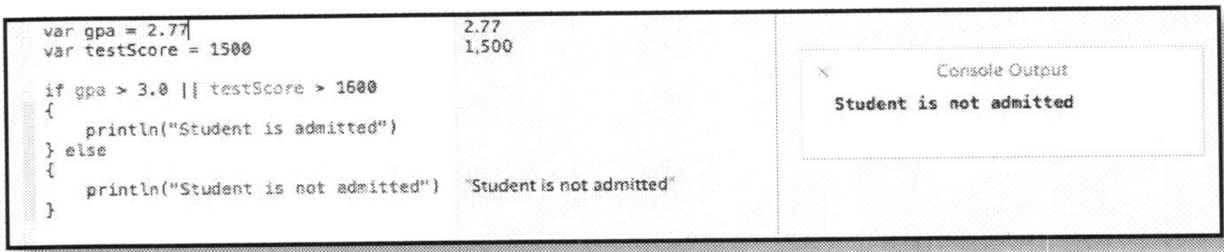

Figure 3-9: Both values are false, so "Student is not admitted" is returned.

Compound conditionals that allow us to test multiple values at the same time are very useful and result in more compact code. Another way to expand on the basic if-statement is through **complex conditionals**. A complex conditional allows us to use a single code block to test against multiple conditions.

Complex Conditionals

Let's consider our prior school admissions example. The school is using a test score and GPA to make decisions, but what if they wanted that test score to be represented by a standard grade letter instead of a number? A complex conditional can handle that situation.

We'll use the "testScore" variable from earlier, but for the sake of the example, change the value to a 100-point-scale. Next, create an if-statement that checks to see if the score is greater than or equal to 90 and, if it is, prints out "A." Do the same for 80, 70, and 60 to determine if a grade is a "B", "C", or "D." Your code should look like this:

```
testScore = 77

if testScore >= 90
{
    println("A")
}
if testScore >= 80
{
    println("B")
}
if testScore >= 70
{
    println("C")
}
if testScore >= 60
{
    println("D")
}
```

When you run this, though, you immediately see the problem. The variable "testScore" is set to the value 77, making the first two if-statements false, but 77 is greater than or equal to both 60 and 70, so both of those if-statements are true. The result is that "C" *and* "D" are output to the console. We could work around this problem using compound conditionals, but there is an easier way.

We can include an if-statement immediately after an else statement in order to create an if-else-if block. When we use the if-else-if technique, the first if-statement is evaluated and if it is true then its code block is executed. After that code block is complete, the remainder of the code in the if-else-if block is skipped. If that first statement is false, then the second statement is evaluated and if that statement is true, its code block is executed. If not, the next statement is tested until a final else statement is reached.

Modify your code so that it looks like the following:

```
if testScore >= 90
{
    println("A")
} else if testScore >= 80
{
    println("B")
} else if testScore >= 70
{
    println("C")
} else if testScore >= 60
{
    println("D")
} else
{
println("F")
}
```

We added the final else statement because we know that if someone didn't achieve any previously tested grades then they must have an "F." Your program's output should match what we see in Figure 3-10:

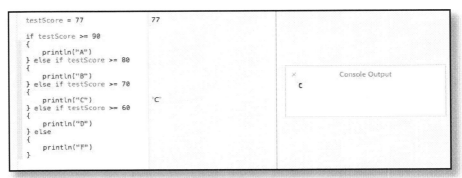

Figure 3-10: A complex conditional tests multiple if-statements in one code block and only executes the code in the first statement that returns true.

You should continue testing your code by changing the value of "testScore" to ensure that you've accounted for all the possibilities. Figures 3-11 and 3-12 show some of the results you can expect.

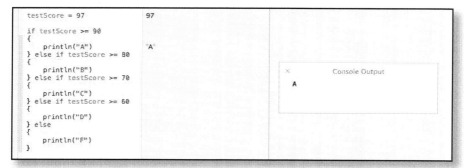

Figure 3-11: In this case, the only if-statement executed is the initial one.

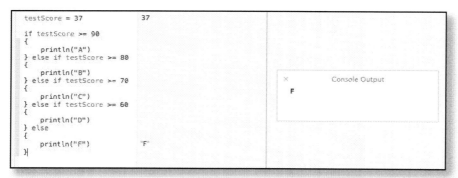

Figure 3-12: In this case, none of the if-statements were true, so the final else-statement was executed.

Compound and complex conditional statements allow you to precisely architect your code so that code blocks only execute in specific, known circumstances.

QUESTIONS FOR REVIEW

1. Which of the following symbols is used to represent "and?"
   a. ##
   b. | |
   c. AND
   d. &&

2. In the following statement:
       a > b | | a > c
   which of the following cases would return true?
   a. a = 1, b = 2, c = 3
   b. a = 2, b = 2, c = 3
   c. a = 2, b = 1, c = 2
   d. a = 2, b = 3, c = 2

3. When is the final else-statement executed in a complex conditional?
   a. Whenever any of the previous if-statements are false.
   b. When all of the previous if-statements are false.
   c. When all of the previous if-statements are true.
   d. It is not executed, it is only there for readability.

4. Only one if-statement in an if-else-if block of code will be run.
   a. True.
   b. False.

3.3 SWITCH STATEMENTS

In the previous section, we looked at complex conditionals and we used them to translate a numerical grade into a letter grade. There is another statement that we could have used there instead of the if-else-if code block, and that's called a **switch statement**.

The switch statement is a single code block that takes a value and then compares it

switch statement

against a number of distinct *cases*. If a case is true, then the switch statement executes the code contained in that particular case before exiting out of the switch code block. If none of the cases are true, then the switch statement would execute a *default* block of code.

We'll test out switch statements in the Xcode playground. Prepare your workspace with a fresh playground and a visible Console Output window. In the last section we were working with grades, so let's continue along those lines. Create a variable "grade" that has as a valid letter grade as a value, for example "A." Now, enter the following:

```
var grade = "A"

switch grade
{
    case "A":
        // What happens if grade is an A
    case "B":
        // What happens if grade is a B
    default:
        // What happens if no case is true
}
```

You now have the basic outline of a switch statement. The statement begins with the keyword "switch" and then is immediately followed by the variable that you're testing against. In the example you just entered, we want to test against "grade." Notice the curly bracket syntax in a switch statement. It's important to note that the entire switch statement is enclosed in one set of curly brackets, as opposed to an if-else-if that is comprised of a number of code blocks in separate curly brackets.

Between the opening and closing curly brackets is the meat of the switch statement. You can see that there are a number of cases that are defined by the keyword, "case." Each case has a value that the switch statement is testing against. We are concerned with a letter grade that is represented by a String variable so our cases are all going to be followed by String. After the cases we have the "default" keyword to define the default case. The default case is what the switch statement will execute if none of the other cases are true. In Swift, switch statements require a default because switch statements are required to be exhaustive. Other programming languages do not require a default case.

> **Tip:** Switch statements in Swift do not require a "break" at the end of each case like some other programming languages do. This is because there is no fall-through after a case executes. A "break" can still be used to exit the switch statement if desired, though.

Now we'll replace the comments with actual code. First, fill out your switch statement so that there are cases that cover every potential letter grade. Once you've done that, have each case print out a different message according to the grade. The default statement should cover the case where a grade that was input is not a valid letter grade, so print out an appropriately expressive message. Your code should look similar to the following example:

```
var grade = "A"

switch grade
{
    case "A":
        println("Outstanding achievement")
    case "B":
        println("Above average
achievement")
    case "C":
        println("Average achievement")
```

```
case "D":
        println("Needs improvement")
case "F":
        println("Failure, Retake Course")
default:
        println("Grade not recognized")
}
```

Once the code is complete, look at your console output. It should appear
like the examples in figures 3-13 and 3-14.

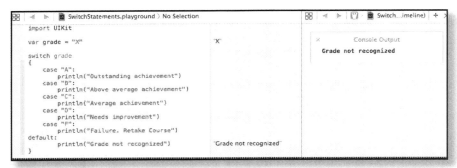

Figure 3-13: This switch statement outputs "Outstanding achievement" because case "A"
was executed.

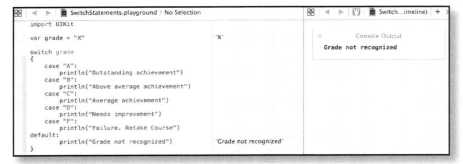

Figure 3-14: In this case, "grade" has the value "X" so the default is executed because "X" is
not covered in any of the specified cases.

Switch statements look for an exact match when they are run. For
example, to the program "A" is not equivalent to "a." If the program were
accepting user input, you should expect that people might use "A" and

"a" interchangeably, so you need to code for that eventuality. We could double the amount of code that we've written by including cases for every uppercase and lowercase letter, or we could use if-statements before the switch-statement to change the value of "grade" into something that we want, but a much easier way is to include more than one value for each case. Swift makes testing against multiple values easy to do.

Change your first case so that it reads as follows:

```
case "A", "a"
    println("Outstanding achievement")
```

Now, change the value of "grade" to "a" and verify your output. You should see "Outstanding achievement" output to the console. In Swift, switch statements can take any number of comma-separated values in each case. Modify the rest of your code to accept either uppercase or lowercase values for "grade."

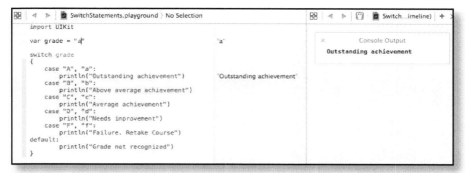

Figure 3-15: Switch statements can test against multiple values for each case.

In our example program we have only used one line of code in each Switch case but Switch cases can contain code blocks with multiple lines. Switch statements allow us to easily and concisely test against a set of values without having to use a lengthy complex if-statement.

1. Does every case in a switch statement require curly brackets?
   a. Yes.
   b. No.

2. When does the default case run in a switch statement?
   a. It will always run.
   b. It will only run when no other cases are true.
   c. It will only run when all other cases are true.
   d. It will never run.

3. Switch statements do not evaluate if a String is uppercase or lowercase when evaluating their value.
   a. True.
   b. False.

4. Is a default block required in a switch statement?
   a. Yes.
   b. No.

3.4 WHILE LOOPS

Loops are a very important concept in programming. A loop is a block of code that is executed multiple times as long as a set condition is true. So far we have dealt with conditionals that will execute code only once, but loops allow us to create code that will run multiple times and that can iterate over sets of data.

The old example of "shampoo bottle instructions" is often used to demonstrate how computers "think." The shampoo example suggests that if a computer was following the instructions on a bottle of shampoo, it would be washing its hair (okay, so the shampoo example also posits that computers have hair) forever, because most shampoo bottles simply instruct, "wash, rinse, repeat." Tired as the trope may be, it can also be quite illustrative.

Once a loop begins, its code will be repeated until the condition that initiated the loop is no longer true. In the shampoo example, the directions never give a condition when the loop should end—there is no "hairClean = true" Boolean declared—so the computer would reach "repeat" and start the loop over. That's something that you, as a programmer, want to avoid.

A **while loop** is a loop where the condition to enter the loop is given when the loop is initialized and that condition is tested again every time the loop's code block ends. This repetition is known as iterating through the loop.

Start a new Xcode playground. The simplest way to utilize a while-loop is with a counter, so declare a variable named "counter" and assign it the value 0.

```
var counter = 0
```

The variable "counter" is the number that we will test against to determine if our loop should be executed. Next, enter the following:

```
while counter < 21
{
    println(counter)
    counter++
}
```

You should already know what most of this example code does. The one new element, the "while" keyword, creates the loop and it is immediately followed by a conditional, just like an if-statement. In our example we want to see if the variable "counter" is less than 21. The curly brackets define the loop code block, just like a switch-statement or if-statement. Within the loop, we're printing out the value of "counter" and using the postfix increment operator to add one to the "counter" value. The increment operator is the key to the loop because it is what allows the loop to end.

Once the code block within a loop is executed, the program returns to the condition and tests it again. If the condition is still true, the code block is executed again. If the condition has become false, the code block is not executed and the program continues. Examine the expected output of the example loop in Figure 3-16:

Figure 3-16: The result of our first simple loop.

Every time our example loop iterates, "counter" is incremented and then "counter" is tested to see if its value is less than 21. In the first iteration, "counter" begins with the value that we initially assigned it, zero, and in the body of the loop "counter" is incremented to one. After the code block is completed, "counter" is checked against the loop condition again and because "counter" is still less than 21, the loop executes. The loop continues until "counter" is equal to 21 and the loop condition is false, at which point the loop ends and the program continues.

Next we're going to explore one of the reasons why loops are so powerful. Underneath your previous example, enter the following code:

```
var testScores = [85,70,92,100]
var i = 0
while i < 4
{
    println(testScores[i])
    i++
}
```

There's an important element here that you haven't worked with yet; it's called an *array*. We will deal with arrays at length in the next chapter, but for our example it's enough to know that an array is a collection that holds a set of values. In the preceding case, we have declared an array called "testScores" and used the brackets to define the array values as the Ints 85, 70, 92, and 100. The values stored in an array are called array members and they are said to be zero indexed. Zero indexed means that the array indexes begin counting from zero. The index of 85 in our example would have the index "0" and the second member in our array, 70, would have the index "1," and so on. When we want to refer to a specific member we use the index in brackets. The first member of our array, with a value of 85, would be referred to as, "testScores[0]."

Array members are ZERO INDEXED

After entering the previous code, your console output should look like figure 3-17:

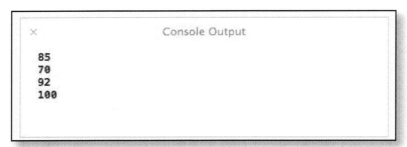

Figure 3-17: The output of our array loop.

The example loop is using the variable "i" as a counter to iterate through every element in our "testScores" array. Recall that we initialized "i" to zero and that the loop is using "i < 4" as its condition. Also, recall that our zero-indexed array has four elements. When we execute the following, "println(testArray[i])," we are instructing the program to print the array member at index location "i" to the console. The initial execution of the loop will therefore be "println(testArray[0])" and then "i" will be incremented. The next iteration of the loop will be println(testArray[1])" and so on until the loop condition is false.

We chose the condition "i < 4" because we know that there are four elements in our array. You might wonder why we did not use "i <= 4" if there are four elements in our array. The reason is because the array is zero indexed, so if we were to use less than or equal to the final value of "i" would be four, meaning that we would be looking for "testArray[4]", which does not exist. You can test this yourself by changing the comparison operator to less than or equal to. You should see an error in your output console like figure 3-18.

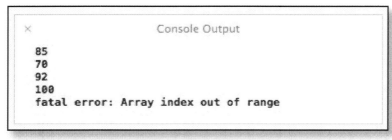

Figure 3-18: The loop asked for an array value that does not exist.

That "index out of range" error tells us that we are asking for a member that the array does not contain. Loops can be very common error points in a program. The "index out of range" error is a fatal error as it is an example of an error that causes a loop to terminate execution. Another potential error when using loops is the infinite loop error. Like our theoretical hairy, hygienic computer, an infinite loop will never be able to finish its execution because its condition will never become false.

So far we have been using the increment operator to iterate through our loops by one. Next, we'll demonstrate a different way to iterate through a loop by counting down from 100 in steps of five. Create a variable named "x" that is assigned the value 100. Since we are counting down, initialize a while-loop that will execute if "x" is greater than -1. In the body of the while-loop, have the program print the value of "x" to the console. Finally, add the following line of code to your loop's code block:

```
x = x - 5
```

The final loop should look like this:

```
var x = 100

while x > -1
{
    println(x)
    x = x - 5
}
```

The code block within the loop is setting the value of "x" to itself minus five. The value of "x" will start the loop as 100 but will be decreased by five after the first iteration, making it 95. Each iteration of the loop will continue to decrement "x" until "x" is negative five, at which point the loop will not execute because "x" will no longer be greater than -1. The output should match what we show in figure 3-19.

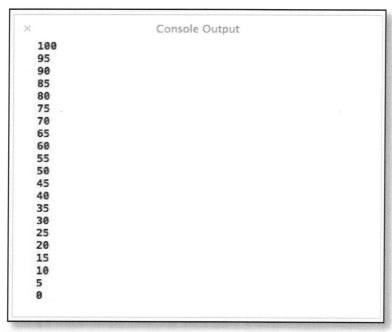

Figure 3-19: Looping down from 100 in steps of 5.

Loops are an integral part of programming. Although the while-loop is tremendously useful, there are multiple loop constructs that can make your coding faster and your code more readable. We'll start going into those other loops in the next sections.

QUESTIONS FOR REVIEW

1. How is a while-loop initialized?
    a. Using the "loop" keyword and a set number of iterations.
    b. Using the "while" keyword and a conditional statement.
    c. Using the "loop" keyword and a conditional statement.
    d. Using the "while" keyword and set number of iterations.

2. Which of the following is a good situation to use a loop?
    a. When you need a block of code to run once no matter what.
    b. When you need to do something specific once a single condition is met.
    c. When you need to iterate through a set of data.
    d. When you have multiple known values to test against.

3. In a while-loop, the condition is tested before the code runs for the first time.
    a. True.
    b. False.

4. Counters used in loops can only count incrementally.
    a. True.
    b. False.

3.5 For Loops

A while-loop is a very commonly used and proven programming concept and it requires three distinct components. First, it requires a value to test, second, it requires a conditional operation to test that value, and finally it requires that the value change at some point so that the conditional will become false and the loop will end. We have been using numbers as our test values and increment or decrement operators as our means of modifying that test value. A **for-loop** contains all of these same basic loop elements, but combines them into an easy-to-use structure.

for-loops

The for-loop takes the pieces of while-loop and puts them all into one line using a specific syntax. Here's an example so you can see how it works:

Create a new Xcode playground and enter the following code:

```
for var i = 0; i < 21; i++
{
    println(i)
}
```

You've already seen everything in this example except for the "for" keyword and the semicolons, so you probably know exactly what's going to happen. Just like the while-loop we started with, we're looping from zero to twenty and outputting the result to the console. What the "for" keyword allows us to do is instruct Swift that the information following the keyword be used to create the loop structure.

In the first code segment, we declared a variable, "i," and then followed that declaration with a semicolon. Loop components in Swift are separated by semicolons.

After the variable declaration, we provide a conditional statement that checks to see if "i" is less than 21. This conditional statement, again, ends in a semicolon. The conditional is what will be tested against to determine if the loop iterates. The final code fragment increments "i." In a for-loop, the final code fragment will always be executed after an iteration is complete and before the test for the next iteration is run, making it the natural place to modify our test value so that we can ensure that the loop will not be infinite.

Verify that everything works by comparing your output to Figure 3-20.

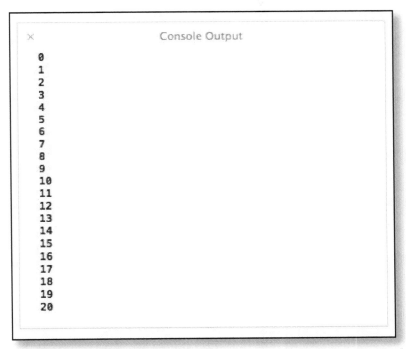

Figure 3-20: Given the same values for the test variable and conditional statement, a for-loop will produce the same results as a while-loop.

For loops can also be used to iterate through arrays in much the same way as while-loops. To demonstrate that arrays can hold different data types, we'll use an example of a shopping list. Create an appropriately named array and assign it the values, "eggs," "milk," "cereal," "flour," "salt," and "sugar." In case you've forgotten the syntax for declaring an array, here is the code:

```
var shoppingList = ["eggs","milk","cereal",
"flour","salt","sugar"]
```

Now type the for-loop that would iterate through the elements in our array. Try it yourself before checking the code below. When you're creating the conditional statement, remember that arrays are zero indexed.

Your code should look like this, although you may have chosen a different name for your test variable:

```
for var x = 0; x < 6; x++
{
    // Do something here
}
```

The loop will iterate six times, with the value of "x" starting at zero and ending at five. Now, output the contents of your shopping list to the console. Recall that we access the value stored at a certain index in an array using brackets and the value of the desired index. Your final code should look like the following:

```
for var x = 0; x < 6; x++
{
    println(shoppingList[x])
}
```

```
× 			Console Output

eggs
milk
cereal
flour
salt
sugar
```

Figure 3-20: If everything went well with your for-loop, you should be looking at this shopping list on your console.

For-loops and while-loops are very similar structures and are often interchangeable. In those situations, which type of loop you choose to use is a matter of personal preference.

QUESTIONS FOR REVIEW

1. Are a for-loop and a while-loop interchangeable?
   a. Yes.
   b. No.

2. A for-loop requires its test value to be incremented in the body of the loop.
   a. True.
   b. False.

3. Which of the following is not a part of the for-loop construct?
   a. Test value.
   b. Condition.
   c. Condiment.
   d. Increment.

4. Can an expression be used when declaring the test value or condition of a for-loop?
   a. Yes.
   b. No.

3.6 FOR... IN LOOPS

A **for-in-loop** is a special type of for-loop that is often used with arrays and can simplify the loop syntax even more.

for-in-loop

With what we know now, if we want to loop through all of the elements of an array we would use the number of elements in the array in our conditional and increment a counter. We would then use that counter to refer to an array index in the body of our loop. This counter technique works, but Swift has a means of looping through an array more easily.

Start a new Xcode playground and create another shopping list array like we did in section 3.5. It can contain any number of items. Once your array is properly declared, enter the following code:

```
println("You need:")
for item in shoppingList
{
    // Do something with item
}
```

The for-in loop instructs Swift to create a constant, called "item," in each iteration of the loop and then assign "item" the value of an array member. Swift knows which member in the array to use because "item" is created and declared as each member in sequence, beginning with index zero and ending with the final index in the array.

In the case of our example, let's confirm that our code is working properly by using the println() function in the body of the loop to output the value of "item" to the console. The shopping list that we created for this example consists of eggs, milk, cereal, flour, cheese, and salad dressing, so our console output looks like figure 3-22.

```
✕                    Console Output
You need:
eggs
milk
cereal
flour
cheese
salad dressing
```

Figure 3-22: Your shopping list will probably be different. Ensure that every element in your array is displayed.

It's easy to see how useful a for-in-loop can be when working with arrays. We no longer have to worry about attempting to access values that are outside of our array or ensuring that our counter variable increments properly. All of that internal work is handled for us by Swift—we just instruct it to provide the data that we want to work with.

For-in loops are very useful for iterating through arrays and they can also be used to iterate through a range of numbers. Enter the following code:

```
for num in 1...6
{
    println(num)
}
```

The for-in-loop is the same as when we worked with an array, but the value passed to it is not an array. Instead it is a new operator called a **range operator**.

Range Operators

→ closed range (...)
→ half-open range (..<)

Range operators are operators that allow you to easily express a range of values. There are two types of range operators: *closed range* (...) and half-*open range* (..<). In our example we've used a closed range operator. Two values are used, a starting and ending value, that define the extent of the range. The range is considered to run from the starting value to the ending value. In order for a range operator to work, the starting value must be less than the ending value. A half-open range operator works the same as a closed range operator but *does not* include the ending value. Half-closed range operators can be useful when working with zero-indexed lists such as arrays.

Considering what you know about how the for-in-loop works and what the range operator does, you should be able to understand how and why the example code works. The constant "num" is declared with values in the range expressed with "1...6" in sequence, meaning that in the first iteration "num" is declared as one, in the second iteration "num" is declared as two, and so on until "num" is declared as six. Since we used an open-range operator in the loop when "num" is declared as six, the loop is run one last time. If it were a closed-range operator, however, the loop would have ended with "num" being declared as five.

After you input the code if you have no errors then your console should look like figure 3-23.

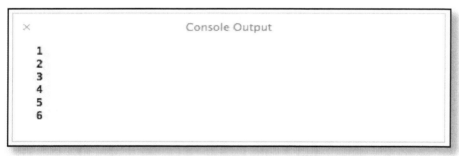

Figure 3-23: Using for-in-loops to iterate through a range of numbers.

Once we have "num" in the body of our loop we can use it in expressions. For example, if we used "println(num * 5)" in place of "println(num)" we would output multiples of five up to the highest ending value of our range, which is six.

```
Console Output
5
10
15
20
25
30
```

Figure 3-24: The value of "num" is multiplied by five before being output to the console.

Swift Fundamentals: The Language of iOS Development

Remember that for-in-loops create a constant and not a variable, so although their value can be used it cannot be changed.

QUESTIONS FOR REVIEW

1. Which of the following statements is true?
   a. For-in-loops use a named variable that is set to a value of an array element.
   b. Elements in an array iterated through by a for-in-loop must be constants.
   c. For-in-loops use a named constant when iterating through array elements.
   d. Range operators do not work with for-in-loops.

2. You must explicitly state how many iterations you want a for-in-loop to go through.
   a. True.
   b. False.

3. What is the difference between an open range operator and a half-closed range operator?
   a. An open range operator iterates through the values between the start and end value but a half-closed range operator iterates through all values.
   b. A half-closed range operator does not iterate through the end value while an open range operator does.
   c. Neither range operator iterates through the final value, but a half-closed range operator also ignores the initial value.
   d. There is no difference between the two.

4 What is the proper syntax for a half-closed range operator?
   a. 1...<9
   b. 1..<9
   c. 1<..9
   d. 1<.>9

CHAPTER 3 LAB EXERCISE

1) Open a new playground called SLA_Lab3. In the text editor, erase any unnecessary code and leave the necessary import statement.

2) Create a multiline comment that lists your name, the date, and the name of the lab assignment (SLA_Lab3).

3) Declare a variable called age. Assign the integer variable an initial value of 39.

4) Create a series of if... else if... and else statements as required to provide the following output for an age value in each of the corresponding ranges:

If age is between...	Output this message with println()
1-11	You're just a kid! Enjoy childhood.
12-19	You'll never be a teenager again. Enjoy these years while they last.
20-29	Get the right education and experience for a career you love.
30-39	Build your career and start saving a little money.
40-49	Time to start thinking about retirement. Hope you're putting money away.
50-59	These can be the most satisfying years of your life. Enjoy your family and friends.
60 +	You're not old, you are just getting started!

5) Test your program. If you don't get the expected result or if the program compiles with an error, debug your code until it functions correctly.

6) Using a while loop, create a pattern of output (using println()) that looks like this:

```
12
24
36
48
60
72
84
96
108
```

7) Using a for loop, display all the numbers under 100 that are evenly divisible by 3. To complete this task, you'll need to use an if statement and the modulus (%) operator. The modulus operator can tell you if a number is evenly divisible by three, like this:

10 % 3 = 1 ← Not divisible by three

9 % 3 = 0 ← Divisible by three

6 % 3 = 0 ← Divisible by three

8) Create an array using the following code:

```
var names = [ "Mark", "Tom", "Jerry",
"Elaine" , "Sue Ellen", "Kerry", "Roger",
"Bob" , "Harry"]
```

9) Create a for...in loop that displays all of the names that are listed in the array.

CHAPTER SUMMARY

In this chapter, we learned what control flow is and why it is so important. We learned about conditionals and used them to control if-statements. We then built on our knowledge of conditions to create complex and compound conditionals. We introduced loops with the while-loop and then expanded on that knowledge with the for-loop and the for-in-loop. We were also introduced to the array type, a very powerful and important concept.

In the next chapter we will go into more detail on the array collection type and why it is so powerful. We will also introduce the dictionary collection type and discuss the power of key-value pairs.

CHAPTER 4

ARRAYS AND DICTIONARIES

CHAPTER OBJECTIVES:

- You will learn what arrays are and how to declare them.
- You will understand the basic array functions Array.Count() and Array.Slice().
- You will utilize advanced array functions to modify array members.
- You will gain an understanding of dictionaries and their declarations.
- You will use dictionary functions to modify, add and remove dictionary members.

4.1 CREATING AND UPDATING ARRAYS

Arrays are a very important data structure in programming. We briefly mentioned arrays in the previous chapter and now we will go into more detail about what arrays are, how they operate in Swift, and how to use them.

arrays

collection type

An array is named and declared in a similar manner to a variable or a constant, but it is a different data type. A Swift array is a **collection type**. A collection type is a data type that stores a collection of other values. In an array, those values are arranged as ordered lists that can be referenced by their location. The other collection type, dictionaries, stores a collection of values according to a unique identifier known as a *key*. We will discuss dictionaries later in this chapter.

We refer to the elements in an array as *members* of that array. In Swift, every member of an array must be of the same type. You can have an array of Ints or an array of Doubles, but you cannot have one array with both Ints and Doubles as members. Since the array has to contain variables of only one type, an array itself can be either implicitly or explicitly declared.

Open a new Xcode playground and enter the following code to create an array declaration:

```
var animals = ["dog","cat","horse"]
```

The "var" keyword is used to declare an array in the same way it is used to declare a variable. The array is then named and the assignment operator is used to set the value of the array members. In Swift, brackets are used to define the values that we want to enter into an array. The use of brackets with arrays is common in many programming languages.

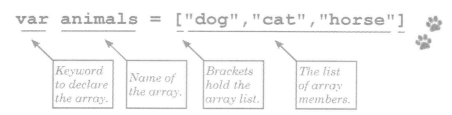

Within the brackets, we have a comma-separated list of values of the same type. Those values are assigned to the members of "animals." In the case of "animals" the array is implicitly typed. Modify the array so that it looks like the following:

```
var animals:[String] =
["dog","cat","horse"]
```

Now we have explicitly declared the array. Note that although the usage of the colon to make an explicit declaration is the same here as it is with variables and constants in array declarations we surround the name of the type with brackets. When we use explicit typing, we need to be explicit about every aspect of the declaration. Here we're instructing Swift to create "animals," and then we're using the colon to indicate that "animals" will be explicitly typed, then the brackets indicate that it is an explicitly typed array, and finally the data type within the brackets indicates the type of the members of the array.

Create an implicitly typed array named "gpas" and set its members as valid GPA floating point numbers. See the following code as an example:

```
var gpas = [3.25,2.55,1.1,3.99,4.0,2.911]
```

Once you're done, check the type using Xcode's code completion bubble. You should be able to verify that "gpas" has been correctly typed as an array of Doubles.

```
var gpas = [3.25, 2.55, 1.1, 3.99, 4.0, 2.911]

   gpas
V  [Double] gpas
```

Figure 4-1: Swift implicitly types arrays just like variables.

We declare variables with the "var" keyword and constants with the "let" keyword, and we know that constants cannot be modified. The same syntax applies to arrays. We can use the "let" keyword to create an array that cannot be modified. When we declare an array with "let" it is not called a constant array but rather an *immutable* array. An immutable array cannot have the values of its members or its size (the number of members in the array) changed. An array that is declared with the "var" keyword can be changed and is called a *mutable* array.

Immutable vs. *mutable* arrays.

In the last chapter we mentioned that arrays are "zero indexed" and explained that zero indexed means that the members of the array are stored as a numbered list that begins with zero. The index is the number that we use to refer to an array member. Go back to your animals array and expand it by adding a few more critters. We used dog, cat, horse, mouse, alligator, rat, alpaca, and elephant.

```
var animals:[String] = ["dog", "cat",
"horse", "mouse", "alligator", "rat",
"alpaca", "elephant"]
```

When we want to access a member of an array we use the name of the array and then we place the index of the member we want to access in brackets. Try the following:

```
println(animals[3])
```

The preceding code would print "mouse" to the console. We can update the value of these members the same way we update the value of any other variable. Change the mouse to a bird:

```
animals[3] = "bird"
```

If we print "animals[3]" now we will output "bird" to the console.

```
println("Change animal 3 from ")
println(animals[3])
println("to")
animals[3] = "bird"
println(animals[3])
```

×	Console Output
	Change animal 3 from mouse to bird

Figure 4-2: We can see how easy it is to update the values of members of arrays.

Because an array is a list of values, it is common to use loops to access array members. In the last chapter we covered loops and went over how to use for-in-loops and for-loops to access array elements. Create a for-loop to access all of the members of your "animals" array and compare your results to figure 4-3. Remember that your array is zero indexed and make sure that you don't attempt to access an array member that does not exist.

```
for var x = 0; x < 8; x++
{
    println(animals[x])
}
```

×	Console Output
	dog cat horse mouse alligator rat alpaca elephant

Figure 4-3: Using a for-loop to access the members of an array.

That's a simple and efficient way to access array members, but we learned something that can be even easier. Use a for-in-loop to achieve the same results.

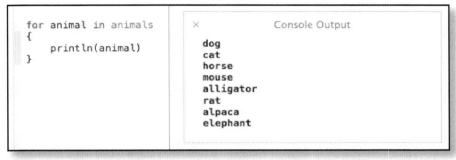

```
for animal in animals
{
    println(animal)
}
```

```
×                    Console Output
dog
cat
horse
mouse
alligator
rat
alpaca
elephant
```

Figure 4-4: The same array accessed with a for-in-loop

You'll notice that in the case of a for-in-loop, your code is much more readable. The members of the array are animals, so by working with the reasonably named value "animal" we have a much better idea of what's going on than if we were to use a syntax like "animals[x]."

Arrays are very useful in Swift and there is much more that we can do with them. Next, we'll learn about two important functions, Array. Count() and Array.Slice().

1. What is the difference between a mutable and immutable array?
   a. A mutable array cannot be accessed through its index while an immutable array can.
   b. A mutable array is zero indexed but an immutable array starts from index one.
   c. An immutable array cannot be modified but a mutable array can.
   d. An immutable array stores Doubles and Floats while a mutable array stores Strings, Ints and Booleans.

2. Which of the following is NOT a correct array declaration?
   a. var myArray = [1,2,3]
   b. var myArray:[Int] = [1,2,3]
   c. let myArray = ["1","2","3"]
   d. var myArray = (1.0,2.0,3.0)

3. An array can contain different variable types.
   a. True.
   b. False.

4. In order to access an array member, what do we need to know?
   a. index
   b. key
   c. value
   d. type

4.2 Array.Count(), Array.Slice()

In the first chapter, we briefly introduced functions and mentioned how useful they could be for organizing code. Some functions can be used in any situation (like the println() function that we've been using to output to the console) but other functions can only work on specific objects. In this section, we'll introduce two array functions, Array.Count() and Array.Slice(), that allow us to get more use out of our Arrays.

Array.Count() is an array function that returns the number of members in an array. Until now, we haven't had to think about determining the length of our arrays because we've been manually

Array.Count()

inputting all of the data. Manually inputting values in code is called "hard-coding" and while it is useful for demonstration purposes, when you begin developing your real applications you'll find that you'll get information from a variety of sources. Often you will not know the exact number of members in the arrays that you're going to be working with.

In a new Xcode playground, explicitly declare an array of Doubles to store GPA values—named "gpas"—and assign its members a set of values:

```
var gpas:[Double] = [3.25,3.11,2.67,1.994,2
.322,3.85,3.91,2.05]
```

If we want to know the number of members of the "gpas" array, we need to use the Array.Count() function. We use the Array.Count() function by appending ".count" to the name of the array, like so:

```
gpas.count
```

GPA
ENTRY
COUNT:
1) *3.25*
2) *3.11*
3) *2.67*
4) *1.994*
5) *2.322*
6) *3.85*
7) *3.91*
8) *2.05*

When you enter that into Xcode, the gutter will display the value of "gpas.count," which is 8. To output that result to the console we would use println():

```
println(gpas.count)
```

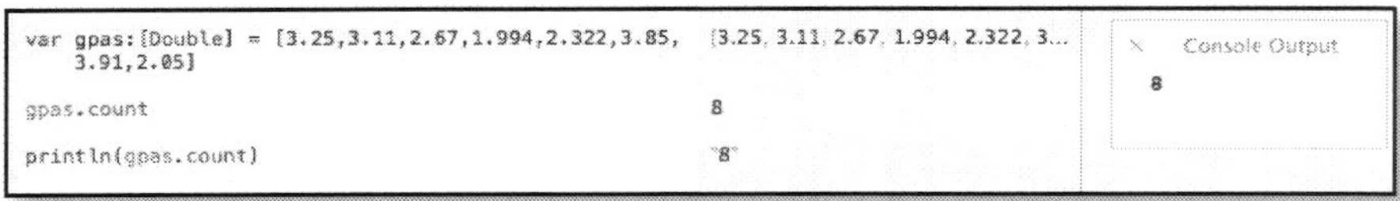

Figure 4-5: Using Array.Count() to determine how many members are in an array.

We can use the returned value from "gpas.count" in many of the same ways that we would use a constant. Using the String Interpolation technique that we learned in chapter two, enter the following code:

```
println("There are \(gpas.count) GPAs in
gpas.")
```

The output will be what you see in figure 4-6.

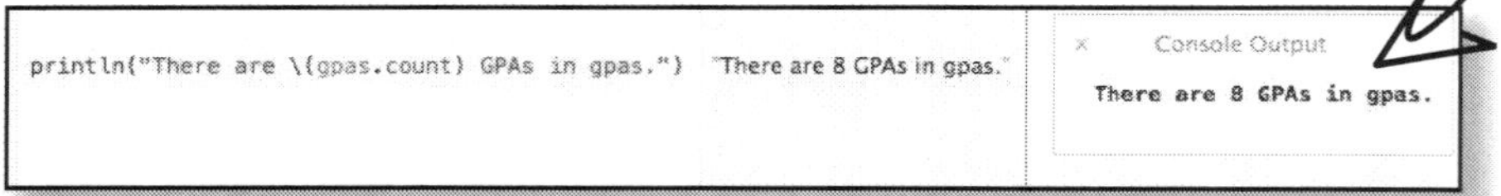

Figure 4-6: String interpolation with the Array.Count() function.

Knowing the number of members in an array is very useful when you're constructing loops. In the following example we'll create a for-loop that will display every member of "gpas" without hard-coding the array length.

```
for var x = 0; x < gpas.count; x++
{
    println(gpas[x])
}
```

You can see in the previous example that we're using the same loop structure that we learned in chapter three but instead of a hard-coded conditional test value we use the value of gpas.count. If you go back and modify the members in your "gpas" array, you'll see that the example for-loop still works and correctly outputs all of the members of "gpa."

> Tip: You describe the index value of an array by saying the array name followed by "sub" and the number of the index. For example, "gpas[3]" would be "gpas sub three."

```
var gpas:[Double] = [3.25,3.11,2.67,1.994,2.322,    [3.25, 3.11, 2.67, 1....    x          Console Output
3.85,3.91,2.05]
                                                                             3.25
for var x = 0; x < gpas.count; x++                                           3.11
{                                                                            2.67
    println(gpas[x])                                  (8 times)              1.994
}                                                                            2.322
                                                                             3.85
                                                                             3.91
                                                                             2.05
```

Figure 4-7: Array.Count() in a for-loop allows you to easily loop through all of the elements of an array of unknown length.

Array.Slice() is an array function that returns a specific range of members of an array. Array.Slice() uses the range operators we learned in chapter three to specify the array members that we are interested in.

Array.Slice()

Using your already populated "gpas" array, enter the following code example:

```
println(gpas[0...3])
```

You can see that we've used the range operator in the brackets where we have been entering our desired index value. Your console output should look like what we have in figure 4-8.

[0...3]

```
var gpas:[Double] = [3.25,3.11,2.67,1.994,2.322,    [3.25, 3.11, 2.67, 1....    x          Console Output
3.85,3.91,2.05]                                                              [3.25, 3.11, 2.67, 1.994]
println(gpas[0...3])                                 [3.25, 3.11, 2.67, 1....
```

Figure 4-8: Using Array.Slice() and range operators to output only certain members of an array.

The output from println() is formatted differently in the previous case because it is displaying multiple members of an array instead of a single member, as we have been doing. If we look at the output, shown in figure 4-8, we can see that the member at index position zero has the value 3.25 and is displayed first in the output console. The following three members displayed in the output correspond to gpas sub one, gpas sub two, and gpas sub three.

You can use Array.Slice() to get any range of members from an array, but it's important to remember that you'll get an error if you attempt to use Array.Slice() for an index that's out of range for a particular array. For example, enter the following code:

```
println(gpas[4...10])
```

You'll get the error shown in figure 4-9 when you attempt the previous example Array.Slice().

Figure 4-9: Array index out of range error when attempting to use Array.Slice() to access an array member that does not exist.

To ensure that the previous error doesn't happen we can combine Array.Slice() with Array.Count() in the following way:

```
println(gpas[4...gpas.count])
```

That gives us the same error, though. The reason for the error is because Array.Slice() returns the number of members in an array and not the number of the final index in the array. In the case of our "gpas" example, the number of members is eight. However, because arrays are zero indexed, the first member of "gpas" has the index value zero and the final member of "gpas" has the index value seven. Thus, the value of "gpas. count," eight, is out of range for the array gpas. We can fix the index out of range error by replacing the closed range operator with the half-open range operator, as shown in the following code:

```
println(gpas[4..<gpas.count])
```

When working with arrays, it is important to remember that arrays are zero indexed. The previous code will resolve the error and your console output should match figure 4-10.

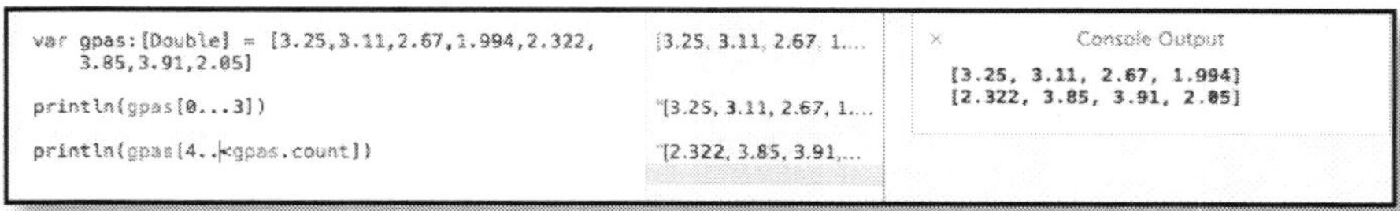

Figure 4-10: Using Array.Count() with Array.Slice() to return a subset of an array.

Array.Count() and Array.Slice() are two important array functions. In the next section, we'll look into what some other array functions are and how to use them.

1. Why is it important to be able to use Array.Count() to get the length of an array?
   a. Because it's annoying to have to count all of the members and enter the number manually.
   b. Because we won't always know the exact length of the arrays we'll be working with.
   c. So that we know how many iterations of for-in loop we're going to need.
   d. Because we don't want our arrays to get too large.

2. Given an Array named "myArray," which of the following is the proper syntax for Array.Count()?
   a. myArray.Count()
   b. count.myArray
   c. count.myArray()
   d. myArray.count

3. What does Array.Slice() allow us to do?
   a. Return a subset of an array.
   b. Return two new arrays "sliced" at a specific index.
   c. Combine two arrays into one larger array.
   d. "Slice off" the final member of an array.

4. Given an array named "myArray" and two integer values "a" and "b," which of the following is the proper syntax for Array.Slice()?
   a. myArray.slice[a...b]
   b. myArray.slice(a...b)
   c. myArray[a...b]
   d. Array.Slice(myArray[a...b])

4.3 ARRAY FUNCTIONS

Now that we know how to use Array.Count() and Array.Slice() we'll look at some other array functions and learn how they can be useful.

Open up Xcode and set up a playground to work on array functions. Make sure that you're able to view the console output. Once your workspace is prepared, create two arrays. Make the first array an explicitly typed array named "teams" and populate it with any number of String elements. Declare the second array as an implicitly typed empty array named "ingredients" but do not set any member elements. Your code should appear similar to the following:

```
var teams:[String] =
["Yankees","Mets","Giants","Jets",
"Nets","Liberty","Red
Bulls","Rangers","Islanders"]
var ingredients = [ ]
```

You might notice in the preceding code that when we declared our "ingredients" array we assigned it empty brackets. Assigning empty brackets instructs Swift to create an array named "ingredients" but does not populate it with any members.

When we discussed Array.Count(), we mentioned that you might not know the specifics of the data that you're working with because you're going to be receiving information from a variety of sources. Array.Count() showed its utility by allowing us to work with arrays of unknown length. A similar question that may come up is whether or not an array has any member elements at all. We can determine if an array is populated or not using the **Array.IsEmpty()** function. Array. IsEmpty() is a function that returns a Boolean value of "true" if the array is empty and "false" if the array is populated.

Array.IsEmpty()

Create an if-else statement to determine if your "teams" array is empty or not and print the result to the console. Your code should look like this:

```
if ingredients.isEmpty
{
    println("The Array is empty")
} else
{
    println("The Array is populated")
}
```

Figure 4-11 shows the result of the previous code. You'll notice that we used the same syntax to determine if an array is empty as we did to use Array.Count() in the previous section. Dot notation allows us to access the functions that are associated with the array element.

Dot Notation

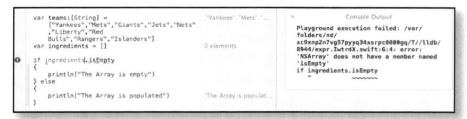

Figure 4-11: The results of testing Array.IsEmpty() on a populated array.

The previous result is not surprising. The result from testing whether or not "ingredients" is empty may surprise you, though. Change "teams. isEmpty" to "ingredients.isEmpty" in the previous example and note the results. They are displayed in figure 4-12.

Figure 4-12: Using Array.IsEmpty() on "ingredients" produces an error message.

When we declared the "ingredients" array we did not assign it any members. In the Swift language, when an array is declared without any members and without being explicitly typed it is created as an *NSArray*. An NSArray is a data type used in the Objective C language that is implemented by Swift in order to support interoperability. We cannot use the same functions with an NSArray as we can with a Swift array.

NSArray

To solve the error we need to explicitly declare "ingredients." By explicitly declaring the type of an array, we are instructing Swift to declare an array of a certain type with no members as opposed to an NSArray. We're going to store cooking ingredients in the "ingredients" array, so the most logical data type for that information would be a String. Change the "ingredients" declaration to an explicit string, as demonstrated in the following code, and check your results against figure 4-13.

```
var ingredients: [String] = []
```

```
var teams:[String] =
    ["Yankees","Mets","Giants","Jets","Nets"
    ,"Liberty","Red
    Bulls","Rangers","Islanders"]
var ingredients:[String] = []

if ingredients.isEmpty
{
    println("The Array is empty")
} else
{
    println("The Array is populated")
}
```

	Console Output
["Yankees", "Mets", "...	The Array is empty
0 elements	
"The Array is empty"	

Figure 4-13: Once "ingredients" is explicitly declare Swift will correctly understand it to be an empty array when using Array.isEmpty().

Now that we know how to determine if an array has any members, we're going to look at how to add members to an array. The simplest way to add members to an array is with **Array.Append()**. Array.Append() takes as a parameter a value of the same type as the Array and includes it as the final element of the array. Enter the following code into your playground:

Array.Append()

```
teams.append("Devils")
println(teams)
```

Again, you're using the dot notation to access the function. As you entered the preceding code into Xcode you likely noticed a code completion bubble as shown here in figure 4-14:

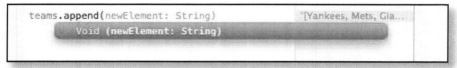

Figure 4-14: When using Array.Append() the code completion bubble reminds you what data type you need to enter.

When you're using the Array.Append() function, the code completion bubble informs you that the function takes a new element as a parameter, that the element has to be of type String, and that the function does not return any data.

The results of the println() function in the earlier code should match what is shown in figure 4-15.

Figure 4-15: Array.Append() appends a new member to the end of an array.

In the output you can see that the array "teams" now includes "Devils" as the value of its final member.

In order to append multiple members to an array, we use an array function known as **array concatenation**. You probably recall concatenation from the section in chapter two about String interpolation. Concatenation in the array context works similarly.

> **array concatenation**

Right now we have an empty String array named "ingredients." First, we're going to use the Array.Append() function to add a member to "ingredients." Then concatenate "ingredients" with another array of Strings:

```
var newIngredients:[String] =
["eggs","sugar","butter"]
ingredients.append("milk")
ingredients += newIngredients
println(ingredients)
```

The concatenation assignment operator is used to concatenate the array "ingredients" with the array "newIngredients." We did not have to create another array, though. We can use the concatenation assignment operator to concatenate an array with a collection of elements using the same syntax as when we declare an array, as in the following example:

```
ingredients += ["eggs","sugar","butter"]
```

Both of those code examples will produce the results shown in figure 4-16.

```
ingredients.append("milk")|
ingredients += ["eggs","sugar","butter"]      ["milk", "eggs", "suga...          ×          Console Output
println(ingredients)                           [milk, eggs, sugar, b...        [milk, eggs, sugar, butter]
```

Figure 4-16: The results of using array concatenation.

So far, we have seen how to add elements to the end of an array, but there are times when we will want to insert elements into an array. **Array.Insert()** allows us to insert a member into a specific index of an array. The Array.Insert() requires two parameters, the value to insert into the array and the index at which it is to be inserted. Enter the following code and pay particular attention to the code completion bubble that appears as you type: **Array.Insert()**

```
ingredients.insert("baking soda",
atIndex:1)
```

```
ingredients.insert( newElement: T , atIndex:
   M  Void insert(newElement: T, atIndex: Int)
   Insert an element at index `i` in O(N).  Requires: `i` <= `count`
```

Figure 4-17: Xcode's code completion bubble gives you information about Array.Insert()'s required parameters.

As you can see in figure 4-17, the code completion bubble gives you important information about the function that you're using. The bubble informs us that the function requires a new element of a specific type and that it requires the "atIndex" keyword followed by an integer value. "T" substitutes for a specific type when using a generic function. We'll learn about generic functions in chapter seven. The integer value that the function requires corresponds to the index where you intend to insert the new element. It must be less than or equal to the value returned from the array's Array.Count() function. In our example, the specific type "T" is substituting for is the String type.

Looking at the code that we entered previously with the information from the code completion bubble in mind, we can see that we have inserted a new String member into "ingredients" at index location one. The result of printing "ingredients" to the console should look like figure 4-18:

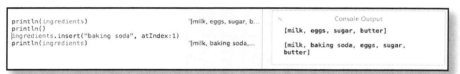

Figure 4-18: Using Array.Insert() inserts a member into an array at a given index location.

Looking at the console output, we can see that before we use Array.Insert() "ingredients[1]" contains the value "eggs" and that after we use Array.Insert() "ingredients[1]" contains the value "baking soda." The other members have all had their index values increased by one to accommodate the new array member. Go ahead and test Array.Insert() with different index values, keeping in mind that the index value you use with Array.Insert() must be less than or equal to "ingredients.count."

There are three array functions that we can use to remove members from an array. The first function removes every element from an array and is called, fittingly enough, **Array.RemoveAll()**. Enter the following code into your Xcode playground:

Array.RemoveAll()

```
ingredients.removeAll()
ingredients.isEmpty
```

You'll notice in the gutter that the evaluated value of "ingredients. isEmpty" is true because using the Array.RemoveAll() function results in an array that retains its type but has no members.

You can also remove specific members from an array. Delete or comment out the preceding example code so that your "ingredients" array retains its members. The first technique we learned to add to an array was the Array.Append() function. The inverse to Array.Append() is **Array.RemoveLast()**. Where Array.Append() adds a member to the end of an array, Array.RemoveLast() removes the final member from an array. Test Array.RemoveLast() with the following code:

Array.RemoveLast()

```
ingredients.removeLast()
println(ingredients)
```

Figure 4-19 demonstrates printing the value of "ingredients" before and after using Array.RemoveLast().

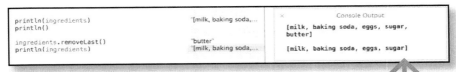

Figure 4-19: Array.RemoveLast() removes the last member from an array.

As you can see, the final member, the String "butter," is removed from the array using the Array.RemoveLast() function.

You should note that if an array is already empty, Array.RemoveLast() will result in an index out of range error. To avoid the index out of range error, you can enclose your Array.RemoveLast() in an if-statement that tests the Array.IsEmpty() function, shown in the following code:

```
if ingredients.isEmpty == false
{
    ingredients.removeLast
}
```

By using the previous code you can be sure that "ingredients.removeLast" will only ever be executed when there are members in the "ingredients" array.

In the same way that we would not always want to append a member to the end of an array, we will not always want to remove the final member of an array. The **Array.RemoveAtIndex()** function allows us to specify the member of an array that we would like to remove. You can use the following example code to try Array.RemoveAtIndex() for yourself.

Array.RemoveAtIndex()

```
ingredients.removeAtIndex(0)
println(ingredients)
```

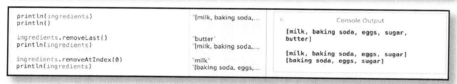

Figure 4-20: Using Array.RemoveAtIndex will remove a member from an array at the specified index location.

As you can see in figure 4-20, using "ingredients.removeAtIndex(0)" removes the array member at index zero. After using this function, "milk" is no longer in the array and "baking soda" becomes "ingredients(0)." You can use Array.RemoveAtIndex() for any valid index in the array.

1. What is the proper usage of Arrays.append()?
    a. Arrays.append() is used to add a member to the beginning of an array.
    b. Arrays.append() appends an empty member to the end of an array.
    c. Arrays.append() is used to add a member to the end of an array.
    d. Arrays.append() combines two arrays into one large array.

2. If Arrays.Insert() is called without the "atIndex:" keyword, the function automatically inserts a member at the end of the array.
    a. True.
    b. False.

3. What syntax would you use to concatenate myArrayA and myArrayB?
    a. myArrayA += myArrayB
    b. myArrayA.concat(myArrayB)
    c. myArrayA = new Array(myArrayA + myArrayB)
    d. You cannot concatenate two arrays.

4. Attempting to use Array.RemoveLast() on an empty array will return an error.
    a. True.
    b. False.

4.4 Creating a Dictionary

The arrays that we have been learning about are one of two collection types in Swift. The other collection type available in Swift is the **dictionary**. A dictionary is similar to an array in that it stores multiple values of the same data type, but it is unique in that those values are stored in assigned key-value pairs using a unique key that is defined by the programmer. Dictionary members do not have a specified order and are looked up based on the key identifier.

Dictionary

key-value pairs

Dictionaries are useful when working with data sets that logically operate in pairs. When data sets operate in pairs they are said to have a one-to-one correspondence. Good examples of one-to-one correspondence would be attributes like a vehicle's top speed or a student's GPA.

To explore how dictionaries work in Swift, we'll begin by creating a dictionary of student names and their GPAs and then we'll loop through our dictionary to output its data to the console. Open up an Xcode playground and enter the following code example:

```
var gpas:[String : Double] =
["Smith":3.01,"Johnson":2.995]
```

The preceding code is an example of an explicit dictionary declaration. The declaration looks similar to an array declaration except that when declaring a dictionary a type is given for both the key and the value. The two type declarations are separated by a colon. In our example we are declaring the key as type String, to store student names, and the value as type Double, to store GPAs. You can see that we use the declared String, Double paradigm to input comma-separated dictionary members on the right side of the assignment operator.

Fill out the "gpas" dictionary using the key value pairs shown in the code that follows:

```
var gpas:[String : Double] = ["Smith":3.01,
"Johnson":2.995,"Thompson":3.112,
"Perry":4.0,"Rockaw":3.1,"Yelvin":2.45]
```

Printing the value of "gpas" to the console using println() will display all of the key value pairs that we have entered. Enter the following code and compare your results to figure 4-21.

```
println(gpas)
```

Figure 4-21: A dictionary printed to the console displays all of the member key-value pairs.

Specific members of a dictionary can be accessed using brackets in the same manner that array members are accessed. Use the code that follows to output the GPAs of Smith and Johnson to the console.

```
println(gpas["Smith"])
println(gpas["Johnson"])
```

The preceding code will use the Strings in brackets to determine the values to display. Figure 4-22 shows you what the output of the preceding code should be.

```
println(gpas["Smith"])          "Optional(3.01)"        Console Output
println(gpas["Johnson"])        "Optional(2.995)"       Optional(3.01)
                                                        Optional(2.995)
```

Figure 4-22: Dictionary values can be accessed using their key in brackets.

For the time being, disregard "Optional." What figure 4-22 shows you is that you can use the key value for dictionaries in the same way that you have been using index values for arrays.

It is possible to loop through all of the data in a dictionary using a for-in loop. Create a for-in loop outline from the following code:

```
for (name, gpa) in gpas
{
    // use "name" and "gpa" as variables in
code here
}
```

As you can see from the preceding code, when using a dictionary the basic structure of the for-in loop remains the same. The inclusion of the comma separated values in parenthesis instructs Swift to use "name" to refer to the key within the loop and "gpa" to refer to the value within the loop. We chose "name" and "gpa" because they are relevant to the data set we are working with, but you can use any valid variable names.

Complete the for-in loop outline by replacing the commented out code with the following println() code:

```
println("\(name): \(gpa)")
```

Using String interpolation we have quickly and easily displayed a very readable output of student GPA data. Figure 4-23 shows the expected output.

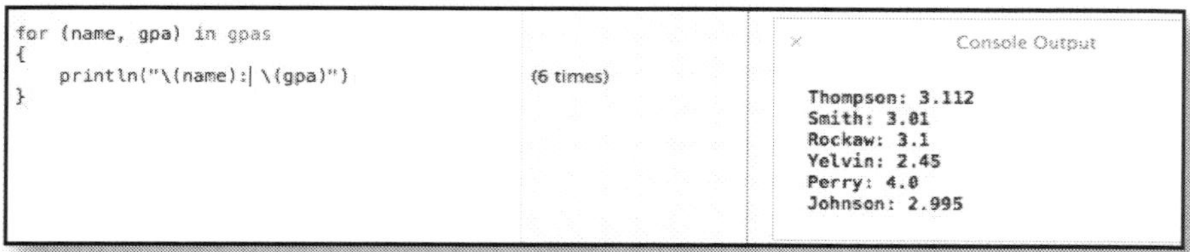

Figure 4-23: A for-in loop is an efficient way to loop through all of the data in a dictionary.

Looking at the data displayed in the console after entering the example code you may have noticed that members are not output in the same order that they were input. In fact, your output is probably in a different order then the output displayed in figure 4-23. For dictionaries, the order of members is irrelevant because they are accessed according to their keys and not according to a specifically ordered Index, like arrays.

The dictionary data type is a very good choice for key-value pairs or data that has a one-to-one correspondence. In the next section we'll look into functions that expand on the utility of the dictionary data type.

QUESTIONS FOR REVIEW

1. What data type is a dictionary?
   a. Variable.
   b. Constant.
   c. Collection.
   d. Function.

2. What is the correct syntax to explicitly declare a dictionary?
   a. var myDictionary:[String] = ["Key","value"; "Key2","value2"]
   b. var myDictionary:[Int;String] = [(1)("value"), (2)("value2")]
   c. var myDictionary:[key(Int):value(String)] = [key(1):value("value"), key(2):value("value2")]
   d. var myDictionary:[Int:String] = [1:"value", 2:"value2"]

3. Dictionaries use an index as well as a key-value pair.
   a. True.
   b. False.

4. How do you access the members of a dictionary in a for-in loop?
   a. for (key, value) in myDictionary
   b. for key, value in myDictionary
   c. for [key, value] in myDictionary
   d. for key: value in myDictionary

4.5 DICTIONARY FUNCTIONS

As with arrays, dictionaries have a number of support functions. Create an Xcode playground and begin by creating a dictionary like the following example:

```
var students =
[1234:"Smith",3456:"Johnson",2211:
"Peters",9876:"Silver",1005:"Gold"]
```

Notice that in the preceding code we implicitly declared the dictionary. Dictionaries, like variables, constants, and arrays, can be either explicitly or implicitly declared. In the preceding example the key is of type Int and the value is of type String. We are supposing that the dictionary "students" contains an integer id number that has a one-to-one relationship with a student's name.

Before we continue, use a for-in loop and println() to output the contents of the dictionary to the console. We will use the initial output as a baseline to understand how the dictionary functions act on the data. Your output should be similar to figure 4-24, but remember that the specific order may be different because dictionaries are not precisely ordered like arrays. You can use the example code that follows to construct your for-in loop.

```
for (idNum, name) in students
{
    Println("\(idNum): \(name)")
}
```

```
var students = [1234:"Smith",3456:"Johnson",   [3456: "Johnson", 12...          ×          Console Output
    2211:"Peters",9876:"Silver",1005:"Gold"]                        3456: Johnson
                                                                    1234: Smith
for (idNum, name) in students                                       2211: Peters
{                                                                   9876: Silver
    println("\(idNum): \(name)")       (5 times)                    1005: Gold
}
```

Figure 4-24: The initial output of our example "students" dictionary.

In order to add a new member to "students," we need to provide the dictionary with a new key-value pair. Enter the following into your playground:

```
students[9675] = "Mettrie"
```

The preceding code creates a member with key 9675 and assigns it the value "Mettrie." Output the modified dictionary and compare it to figure 4-25.

Figure 4-25: Our "students" dictionary after adding a value.

We can modify the value of a key-value pair by using the key in a similar manner. Just as we modify a variable using an assignment operator, we can modify a key-value pair using the dictionary name, brackets, the known key, the assignment operator, and a new value. Enter the following example before your for-in loop:

```
students[1234] = "Berg"
```

Once you've entered this example code, output "students" to the console. Your output should be similar to figure 4-26.

students[1234] = "Berg"|	(Some "Berg")		Console Output

for (idNum, name) in students
{
    println("\(idNum): \(name)")
}
	(6 times)		3456: Johnson
			1234: Berg
			2211: Peters
			9876: Silver
			1005: Gold
			9675: Mettrie

Figure 4-26: Modifying a dictionary value by using the assignment operator.

While the assignment operator allows us to directly modify a value in a dictionary's key-value pair, there is a specific dictionary function that can be used instead. The modification function is called **Dictionary.UpdateValue()**. Dictionary.UpdateValue() also allows us to update the value of a key-value pair, but it returns the original value of the member that was updated. Dictionary.UpdateValue() is easier to understand in practice.

Enter the following code into Xcode before your for-in loop:

```
var replacedValue = students.
updateValue("Uvalde", forKey: 2211)
println("The replaced value is \
(replacedValue)")
```

While you're entering the preceding code, you may have noticed a code completion bubble offering suggestions for "students.updateValue()." Those suggestions are shown in figure 4-27.

```
var replacedValue =
    students.updat
    forKey: (Key )
                    M  Value? updateValue(value: Value, forKey: Key)

for (idNum, name)    Update the value stored in the dictionary for the given key, or, if
{                    they key does not exist, add a new key-value pair to the dictionary.

    println("\(idNum): \(name)")                    (6 times)
}
```

Figure 4-27: The code completion bubble for Dictionary.UpdateValue() informs you of the required parameters.

The code completion bubble shown in figure 4-27 lets you know that in order to use Dictionary.UpdateValue() you need a value to pass to the member. Our code passes the value "Uvalde" and uses the "forKey" keyword to pass the key 2211. The "forKey" keyword is required for Dictionary.UpdateValue().

You may also note that to the left of the function name is "Value?" rather than "Void." That "Value?" is informing you that Dictionary.UpdateValue() can return a value. Looking at the output, shown in figure 4-28, will show you what the returned value is.

```
var replacedValue =                         [Some "Peters"]
    students.updateValue("Uvalde", forKey:                      Console Output
    2211)
println("The replaced value is \         The replaced value i...    The replaced value is
    (replacedValue)")                                                Optional("Peters")
for (idNum, name) in students                                       3456: Johnson
{                                                                   1234: Berg
                                                                    2211: Uvalde
    println("\(idNum): \(name)")          (6 times)                 9876: Silver
}                                                                   1005: Gold
                                                                    9675: Mettrie
```

Figure 4-28: The console output shows what was returned from Dictionary.UpdateValue().

Looking at your console output, you can see that the variable "replacedValue" was assigned the original value of the member whose key was passed to Dictionary.UpdateValue(). Dictionary.UpdateValue() then modified the value of that key-value pair.

Using Dictionary.UpdateValue() instead of the assignment operator to modify the values in a dictionary allows you to retain the original value and store it or use it again as needed. With a hard-coded dictionary, as we are using in the example, knowing the value that we modified might not be a concern, however it can be vital when working with unknown data.

There are similar techniques to remove members from a dictionary. First, enter the following code before your for-in loop:

```
students[1005] = nil
```

The preceding code uses a new keyword, "nil." Using "nil" points the key to nothing, effectively causing the dictionary to remove the key. Note the results from the console output in figure 4-29.

```
students[1005] = nil                      nil
                                                                   Console Output
for (idNum, name) in students                                       3456: Johnson
{                                                                   1234: Berg
                                                                    2211: Uvalde
    println("\(idNum): \(name)")          (5 times)                 9876: Silver
}                                                                   9675: Mettrie
```

Figure 4-29: The result of setting "students[1005]" to "nil."

The value of "students[1005]" was the String "Gold," but setting it to "nil" removes it from the dictionary. Using "nil" we can remove members from a dictionary, but there is another method that is similar to Dictionary.UpdateValue().

Dictionary.RemoveValueForKey()

Dictionary.RemoveValueForKey() is a dictionary function that removes a member from a dictionary but returns its value in much the same way that Dictionary.UpdateValue() did. To test Dictionary.RemoveValueForKey(), change "students[1005] = nil" to the following:

```
var deletedValue = students.
removeValueForKey(1005)
println("The deleted value is \
(deletedValue)")
```

Figure 4-30 shows the expected output of the preceding code block.

Figure 4-30: Dictionary.RemoveValueForKey() removes a member from a dictionary and returns that member's value.

In the preceding code we created the variable "deletedValue" and assigned to it the value of the member that was removed from the "students" dictionary. Note that we did not have to use a keyword when we passed the key to Dictionary.RemoveValueForKey(). The value was confirmed in the output as the String "Gold" and the output of the remaining members of "students" no longer includes key 1005. As with Dictionary.UpdateValue(), Dictionary.RemoveValueForKey() allows us to retain the value and store it or use it as needed.

QUESTIONS FOR REVIEW

1. What syntax would correctly add a new member to the dictionary "myDictionary?"
   a. myDictionary.append(4321,"Jones")
   b. myDictionary += [4321:"Jones"]
   c. myDictionary[4321] = "Jones"
   d. myDictionary.addValue("Jones", forKey:4321)

2. Modifying a dictionary member using the assignment operator is a valid technique.
   a. True.
   b. False.

3. What does Dictionary.UpdateValue() do?
   a. It updates the value of a dictionary member and returns Void.
   b. It updates the value of a dictionary member and returns the key.
   c. It updates the value of a dictionary member and returns the original value.
   d. It updates the key of a dictionary member.

4. Which are NOT ways to remove a member from a dictionary? (Choose all that apply.)
   a. myDictionary[1234] = nil
   b. myDictionary.delete(1234)
   c. myDictionary.removeValueForKey(1234)
   d. myDictionary -= myDictionary[1234]

CHAPTER 4 LAB EXERCISE

1) Open a new playground called SLA_Lab4. In the text editor, erase any unnecessary code and leave the necessary import statement.

2) Create a multiline comment that lists your name, the date, and the name of the lab assignment (SLA_Lab4).

3) Create an array named shoppingList which includes the following members:

Eggs
Milk
Soda
Butter
Bread
Yogurt
Cheese
Beer
Chicken
Apples
Pears

Make sure you initialize the array with var. (You'll be making changes to the array members, so you want to make sure the array is mutable.)

Once you create the array, println() the 4th and 7th members of the array.

4) Replace "Beer" in the array with the value "Wine."

5) Using the Array.Count() function, print the following sentence:

```
There are X items on the shopping list.
```

Insert your Count() function where the X is to output the number of items in the array.

6) Create a dictionary with the following key/value pairs

Key	Value
JFK	John F. Kennedy International Airport
LGA	LaGuardia Airport
ORD	Chicago O'Hare International Airport
LAX	Los Angeles International Airport
BDL	Bradley International Airport
AUS	Austin-Bergstrom International Airport
FLL	Ft. Lauderdale International Airport
EWR	Newark Liberty International Airport
DCA	Ronald Reagan Washington National Airport

7) Using a for...in loop, output the airport abbreviation and airport name in the following format:

```
KEY is the abbreviation for VALUE
```

8) Add the following data to the dictionary:

PVD	TF Green Airport
SFO	San Francisco International Airport

9) Repeat step 7, using a for...in loop to output the dictionary values.

CHAPTER SUMMARY

In this chapter, we learned about the collection data types, arrays and dictionaries. We learned that arrays are best for storing lists of data and that their data is referenced using an index value, whereas dictionaries are most effective when using data elements that have a one-to-one relationship because the information is stored in key-value pairs. We gained an understanding of the functions that allow us to edit arrays and dictionaries and used practical examples to learn the function syntax.

Going forward, we will further utilize the collection data types as well as all of the knowledge we have gained so far in order to expand the functionality of our programs. In chapter five we will delve into functions, learn how to create our own functions, and explore the utility of functional programming in Swift.

CHAPTER 5

FUNCTIONS

CHAPTER OBJECTIVES:

- You will learn what functions are and why they are so useful.
- You will be able to declare your own functions and better organize your code.
- You will learn how to send information to functions using arguments and how to process that data within a function.
- You will understand how to return data from a function and use that data later in your code.
- You will learn about variable scope.
- You will gain an understanding of nested functions and how using nesting you can further improve your code organization.

5.1 FUNCTION DEFINITION AND FUNCTION CALLS

In chapter four we learned how arrays and dictionaries have built-in functions that we are able to use. In this chapter, we will go over what functions are, why they are such an important programming concept, and how to create and use your own functions.

A **function** is a named and encapsulated code block that you intend to use multiple times. Functions can take parameters and can return values, but they do not have to. When we use a function we are said to have made a **function call**. A function call instructs the program to execute the code in the function's code block, and then continue executing the code after the function call.

We will begin exploring functions by using two simple code blocks that will be very familiar. In a new Xcode playground, enter the following code:

function

function call

```
func sayHello()
{
    println("Hello there!")
}
```

In the preceding code example we have a very simple function declaration. The **func** keyword in Swift begins the function declaration. Immediately following is the name assigned to the function. The name is what we will use to refer to the function using function calls and is written in camel case. After the name we have an empty set of parenthesis. If our function takes arguments, we define them within those parentheses. We will discuss function arguments in the next section. The final part of a function is a code block defined by curly brackets, similar to what we have seen with conditional statements.

func

The code contained within the curly brackets is the code block that will execute when the function is called. Right now, your console output should look like this:

```
func sayHello()
{
    println("Hello there!")
}
```
Console Output

Figure 5-1: A simple function declaration.

You might be wondering why the console output is empty even though we used println(). The reason is

No output yet...

that the code block in the curly brackets has not been executed yet. In the same way that the code in a conditional statement will not be executed until its condition returns "true," the code in a function will not be executed until that function is called. Enter the following code into your playground, underneath your function declaration:

```
sayHello()
```

While you were typing the example code you might have noticed the code completion bubble pop up. Xcode is aware of your function and suggests it in much the same way that it has been suggesting the built-in functions for arrays and dictionaries. See figure 5-2 for an example of the code completion bubble.

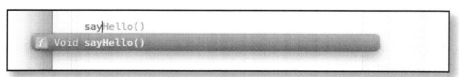

Figure 5-2: Xcode's code completion bubble suggests the function that we've just declared in the same way that it suggests a built-in function.

Once you've entered your function call you should have output in your console like what is shown in figure 5-3.

Figure 5-3: The function "sayHello()" outputs text to the console when called.

Every function that we declare needs to have a unique name and we can declare more than one function in a program. Below the "sayHello()" function that you've declared, enter the following code:

```
func sayGoodbye()
{
    println("Goodbye!")
}
```

The preceding code uses the same syntax as "sayHello()" to declare a function named "sayGoodbye()" that operates in a very similar manner. Below the "sayHello()" function call in your code, create multiple "sayGoodbye()" function calls. Your output should match the output shown in figure 5-4.

```
func sayHello()
{
    println("Hello there!")          "Hello there!"
}
func sayGoodbye()
{
    println("Goodbye!")              (3 times)
}

sayHello()
sayGoodbye()
sayGoodbye()
sayGoodbye()
```

```
×                    Console Output
Hello there!
Goodbye!
Goodbye!
Goodbye!
```

Figure 5-4: The power of functions come from their ability to be called multiple times, making it simple to reuse code.

You can see that we have output "Goodbye!" multiple times by making multiple calls to the "sayGoodbye()" function. The examples that we've been working with are simple, but you can imagine how powerful functions are when they reuse complex code.

> **Tip:** Many programmers keep libraries of common functions that they have created and know that they will be using in the future. For example, someone working in e-commerce might have a library of functions that handle currency conversions and calculations.

There is something else to note about functions in Swift. Remove the function calls from your code and reenter them before you declare your function. Look at the output that you get to the console, it should match figure 5-5.

Figure 5-5: Function calls working prior to the function being declared.

Up until now we have only seen code being executed in the order it is written. When developing in Swift, though, you do not have to declare your function before you make a function call, but the function does have to be declared somewhere in your code. Separating out functions can allow you to better organize your code.

1. Functions allow us to reuse blocks of code.
   a. True.
   b. False.

2. In order to create a function called "myFunction," what syntax would you use?
   a. function myFunction()
   b. var myFunction():Function
   c. func myFunction()
   d. let myFunction():Function

3. Where does a function need to be declared in order for it to be used in a program?
   a. Immediately before the first time the function is called.
   b. All functions must be declared at the beginning of the program.
   c. A function may be declared anywhere in the code.
   d. In a separate "functions" file.

4. When is the code within a function executed?
   a. Function code is executed only when the function is called.
   b. Function code is executed when the function is first declared and again whenever it is called.
   c. Function code is only executed when its conditional statement evaluates to "true."
   d. Function code is executed every Thursday at 4:56 in the afternoon, GMT.

5.2 Functions that Take Arguments

Using functions to execute code blocks is very powerful, but functions gain substantially more utility when we are able to pass information to them to be processed. We have passed information before with dictionary and array functions as well as with the println() function. Now we're going to learn how to build our own functions to process passed information.

When we pass information to functions, we say that we are passing **arguments** or **parameters**. Arguments and parameters refer to the information that we want a function to process and are passed in variable form. Because we can pass multiple arguments of different types to a function, in the function declaration we have to name them and define their type.

arguments

parameters

Open up a new Xcode playground and enter the following basic parameterized function declaration:

```
func sayGreeting(name: String)
{
println("Hello, \(name)")
}
```

The function declaration is very similar to our earlier "sayHello()" function, only instead of empty parentheses we have a statement that looks like an explicit variable declaration. The similarity is because the parameter is passed to the function as a variable. We need to name that variable for use in the function and also define the type of variable that is expected. In this case, "sayHello()" is taking a String variable as a parameter and referring to it as "name" for use within the function's code block.

Enter the following code to call the function that we've just created.

```
sayGreeting("Mark")
```

Once you've entered the preceding code, you should see console output like in figure 5-6. The String "Mark" is being sent to the function "sayGreeting()" as an argument that is assigned to the variable "name." The println() command uses "name" when it outputs to the console.

```
func sayGreeting(name: String)
{
    println("Hello \(name)")              "Hello Mark"
}

sayGreeting("Mark")
```
```
×                    Console Output
Hello Mark
```

Figure 5-6: Using parameters allows us to process information in the functions we declare.

You can pass any String value to the "sayGreeting()" function. In figure 5-7 we have passed another name to the function as an example. Use your name in the function to verify that the parameter is passing correctly.

```
func sayGreeting(name: String)
{
    println("Hello \(name)")              (2 times)
}

sayGreeting("Mark")
sayGreeting("Tom")
```
```
×                    Console Output
Hello Mark
Hello Tom
```

Figure 5-7: Functions that take parameters produce different results depending on the information passed to them.

Functions can also take multiple arguments. To demonstrate multiple arguments, we'll create a function that solves for the hypotenuse of a right triangle. The Pythagorean Theorem states that the sum of the square of the two shorter sides of a

The Pythagorean Theorem:

$$a^2+b^2=c^2$$

right triangle is equal to the square of the longest side, or hypotenuse. We represent this as $a^2+b^2=c^2$ where "a" and "b" are the lengths of the short sides of the right triangle and "c" is the length of the hypotenuse. We will use this theorem in our function. Enter the following function declaration:

```
func solveHypot(sideA: float_t, sideB:
float_t)
{
    // Math goes here
}
```

As you can see in the preceding code, we are using the same syntax as in our "sayGreeting()" function but instead of having a single parameter we are using a comma-separated list of multiple parameters. Erase the comment and enter the following code:

```
var sideC = (sideA * sideA) + (sideB *
sideB)
sideC = sqrt(sideC)
println(sideC)
```

The first line of the preceding code declares a "sideC" variable and assigns it the result of "sideA" multiplied by itself and then added to "sideB" multiplied by itself. We know that the equation will be valid because we know that the values of "sideA" and "sideB" are both of type Float. The next line uses "sideC" with one of Swift's built-in math functions, "sqrt()." The sqrt() function returns the square root of the value that is passed to it. We have evaluated "sqrt(sideC)" on the right side of the assignment operator so its result is assigned to sideC. In figure 5-8 you can see the code completion bubble from the sqrt() function.

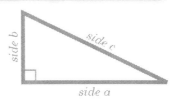

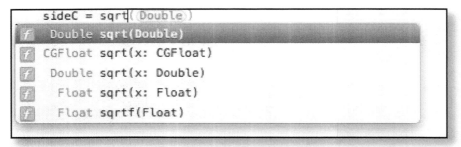

Figure 5-8: sqrt() is one of Swift's built-in math functions.

Once we have done the math we know that the value of "sideC" is the length of the hypotenuse, so we print that value to the console. Now that you've created the "solveHypot()" function, use the following code to verify that it works:

```
solveHypot(12,9)
```

While you are entering the previous code you might have noticed another code completion bubble. Xcode is aware of the function and it is also aware of the variable types that the function takes as parameters, so in the code completion bubble it reminds you what values you need to pass to "solveHypot()." The code completion bubble is shown in figure 5-9.

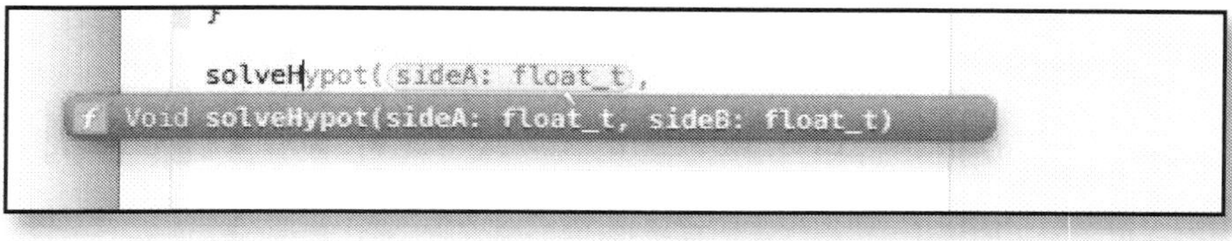

Figure 5-9: Xcode's code completion bubble pops up to remind you what you need to pass to the function that you've created. In the case of "solveHypot()" we need to pass two Float values.

Once the aforementioned code example is entered into your playground you should see the value of the hypotenuse in the console window. If you call "solveHypot()" again with different values, you'll see that the function again correctly outputs the answer.

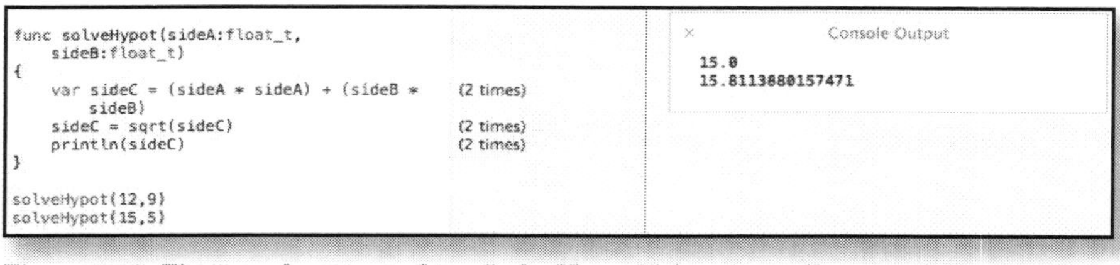

Figure 5-10: The console output of two "solveHypot()" function calls using different values.

Arguments substantially increase the utility of functions. In the next section, we'll learn how to use functions to return values so that we can use the processed information later in our code.

1. What is the purpose of arguments?
   a. Arguments allow us to pass information to functions to be processed.
   b. Arguments are used to modify the name of a function.
   c. Arguments change the order that functions are executed.
   d. Arguments are not useful to functions.

2. Which of the following is a proper function declaration?
   a. func myFunction(var arg1, var arg2)
   b. func myFunction[arg1, arg2]
   c. func myFunction(arg1: Int, arg2: String)
   d. func myFunction(arg1:arg2)

3. Functions can take more than one argument.
   a. True.
   b. False.

4. Xcode's code completion bubbles will ignore our functions.
   a. True.
   b. False.

5.3 FUNCTIONS THAT RETURN VALUES

In section 5.2, we saw how functions take arguments and use them in their code blocks by creating a function that output the length of the hypotenuse when given the lengths of the shorter two sides of a right triangle. There are also circumstances where instead of outputting that data, we want to use it again within the program. In a case where we want to use the result of a function, we have to create a function with a **return value**.

return value

A return value in a function is the value that is the result of the processing that occurs within the function's code block. To demonstrate function returns, we'll create a simple program that returns one out of a random selection of greetings. First, create a new Xcode playground and then enter the following function declaration:

```
func randomInt(min:Int,max:Int)->Int
{
    // Code goes here
}
```

The preceding function declaration creates a function named "randomInt" and it takes two arguments, variables of type Int named "min" and "max." Next, there is a symbol that looks like an arrow. The return symbol (->) establishes that we expect "randomInt()"to return a value. The type after the symbol defines the type that we intend to return. Replace the comment with the following code. Don't worry if you don't understand all of it yet.

```
return min + Int(arc4random_
uniform(UInt32(max - min + 1)))
```

The preceding code begins with the keyword "return" which informs Xcode that the value the statement results in will be the function's return value. We are using Swift's built-in arc4random_uniform() function, which returns a random Int value between zero and the value of the argument passed to it, as the basis of our statement. The final result of the statement will be a random number between "min" and "max."

Call the function that you've just created and pass it any two values, making sure that "min" is less than "max." Use the following code as an example:

```
          Min | Max
           ↓   ↓
randomInt(0,10)
```

Although your gutter will display a result, the value is not being displayed on the console or used by your program. The result of your function call is an Int and the println() function that we have been using can take an Int as a parameter. Use your function call as println()'s parameter to see how that returned value is handled when it is used as a parameter. Figure 5-11 shows the results that you can expect.

```
println(randomInt(0,10))
```

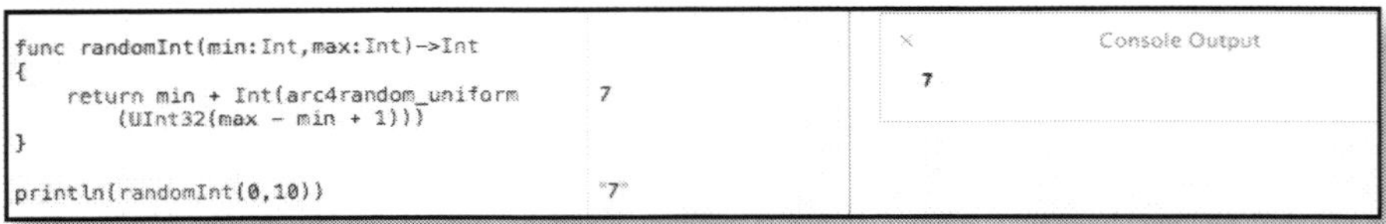

func randomInt(min:Int,max:Int)->Int {			✕	Console Output
return min + Int(arc4random_uniform	7		7	
(UInt32(max - min + 1)))				
}				
println(randomInt(0,10))	"7"			

Figure 5-11: Using println() to output the return value of a function to the console window.

The example code has taken the value that was returned from "randomInt()" and then passed it to println(). You can see that println() treats it as it would any other valid value. There is much more that we can do with returned values from functions. The following code will create the outline for our random greetings function.

```
func randomGreeting()->String
{
    // Code goes here
}
```

If you allow Xcode to evaluate the previous code fragment you'll get an error, as seen in figure 5-12.

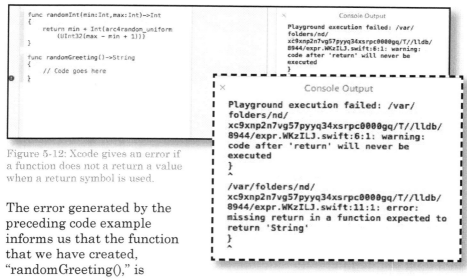

Figure 5-12: Xcode gives an error if a function does not a return a value when a return symbol is used.

The error generated by the preceding code example informs us that the function that we have created, "randomGreeting()," is supposed to provide a return value but that we have not yet coded it. Replace the comments in the code with the following:

```
return ""
```

In the previous code we have merely returned an empty String because we know that the "randomGreeting()" function will eventually return a String.

```
func randomInt(min:Int,max:Int)->Int
{
    return min + Int(arc4random_uniform
        (UInt32(max - min + 1)))
}

func randomGreeting()->String
{
    return ""
}
```

Figure 5-13: Xcode expects a String as a return value and will accept even an empty String.

Once we have updated the code and eliminated the error, we can create a String array of possible greetings. The following example code shows some greetings:

```
var greetings = ["Hello,
there!","Greetings!","Good Day!","Good
Morrow!","Hey!","Yo!"]
```

We have created an array so we know that all of the members of "greetings" are organized in a zero-indexed list. Our "randomInt()" function from before will provide us with a suitable random number that we can use as an index reference for our "greetings" array. Consider how you would solve the problem, and compare your solution to our code example that follows:

```
var greetingNumber = randomInt(0,5)
```

We know that our "greetings" array has six elements and, because it is zero-indexed, we know that any random number between zero and five, inclusive, will be a valid index. We use the return value of our "randomInt()" function with the parameters zero and five to get a valid index value and then assign it to the variable "greetingNumber." We now have a number that can act as an index reference for our array. Change the return statement to return the appropriate String value, as shown in our code example:

```
return greetings[greetingNumber]
```

The previous example uses the value of the "greetingNumber" variable that was returned from "randomInt()" as the index reference to a member of the "greetings" array. The String value of that array member is used as the return value of the function. Figure 5-14 shows what we can expect once we use println() to output that value to the console:

```
func randomInt(min:Int,max:Int)->Int
{
    return min + Int(arc4random_uniform      2          Good Day!
        (UInt32(max - min + 1)))
}

func randomGreeting()->String
{
    var greetings = ["Hello,
        there!","Greetings!","Good           ["Hello, there!", "Gre...
        Day!","Good Morrow!","Hey!","Yo!"]
    var greetingNumber = randomInt(0,5)      2
    return greetings[greetingNumber]         "Good Day!"
}

println(randomGreeting())                    "Good Day!"
```
```
Console Output

Good Day!
```

Figure 5-14: Our "randomGreeting()" function returns a string that println() can output to the console.

We are using a hard-coded array in the preceding example, so we know exactly what the limits on our index are going to be. We can, instead, use a technique that we learned in section 4.2 to modify the code to account for unknown array sizes. Modify the declaration of "greetingNumber" to match the following code:

```
var greetingNumber = randomInt(0,greetings.
count-1)
```

The preceding code uses the returned value from the Array.Count() function as one of the arguments for our "randomInt()" function. You'll note that we had to modify the returned value from Array.Count() to account for the fact that arrays are zero indexed. The example shows how versatile function parameters and returned values are.

```
func randomInt(min:Int,max:Int)->Int
{
    return min + Int(arc4random_uniform      1          Greetings!
        (UInt32(max - min + 1)))
}

func randomGreeting()->String
{
    var greetings = ["Hello,
        there!","Greetings!","Good           ["Hello, there!", "Gre...
        Day!","Good Morrow!","Hey!","Yo!"]
    var greetingNumber = randomInt(0,
        greetings.count-1)                   1
    return greetings[greetingNumber]         "Greetings!"
}

println(randomGreeting())                    "Greetings!"
```
```
Console Output

Greetings!
```

Figure 5-15: The "randomGreeting()" function uses the output of the "randomInt()" to generate its return value, and "randomInt()" uses the returned value from the Array.Count() function as a parameter.

Having the ability to send data to functions, process the data, and then return the result is very powerful. As we continue to write more complicated functions, we will find that we need to declare and use variables inside the functions. In the next section we will discuss using variables within functions and variable scope.

 QUESTIONS FOR REVIEW

1. Why is it useful to return values from functions?
   a. In order to use the function's resulting data in our program.
   b. So that we can ensure that the function is implemented properly.
   c. Because functions require some return value.
   d. To output the function's result to the console.

2. A function can take parameters and also return a value.
   a. True.
   b. False.

3. We cannot assign the returned value from a function to a variable.
   a. True.
   b. False.

4. What is the correct syntax for a function that returns a value?
   a. func myFunction() RETURNS String
   b. String func myFunction()
   c. func myFunction()->String
   d. func myFunction(->String)

5.4 VARIABLE/CONSTANT SCOPE AND FUNCTIONS

The **scope** of a variable in programming refers to the parts of the program where a variable is visible. In this section we'll discuss how scope relates to the variables, constants, and functions that we've been working with.

scope

Open Xcode and set up a new playground. We'll first examine scope for variables and constants. Declare a variable named "score" and assign it the value 1000, then declare a constant named "width" and assign it the value 10.55. Using String interpolation, print the values of "score" and "width" as shown in the following code example:

```
var score = 1000
let width = 10.55

println("Outside function variable: \
(score)")
println("Outside function constant: \
(width)")
```

There's nothing new in the example code. You should see two lines of output in the console confirming the values of both "score" and "width." Now, create a simple function, "myFunc()," that doesn't take any parameters and that returns void. A function that returns void is a function that does not provide a value to its caller. In the "myFunc()" code block, output the values of "score" and "width" as follows:

```
println("Inside function variable: \
(score)")
println("Inside function constant: \
(width)")
```

Just below your original println() commands, call "myFunc()." The output of the function call should match what we have in figure 5-16.

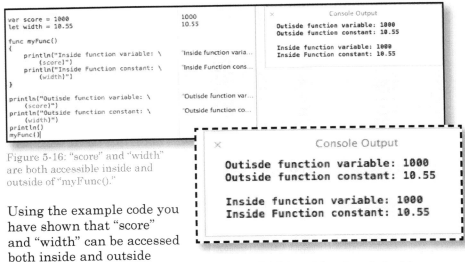

Figure 5-16: "score" and "width" are both accessible inside and outside of "myFunc()."

Using the example code you have shown that "score" and "width" can be accessed both inside and outside "myFunc()." The scope of "score" and "width" is said to be **global** because they are visible and accessible anywhere in the program.

Within "myFunc()" create a variable called "funcVar" and assign it the value 55. While still in the "myFunc()" code block enter the following code:

global

```
println("Inside function funcVar: \
(funcVar)")
```

Your console output will have changed to include the value of "funcVar", as shown in figure 5-17.

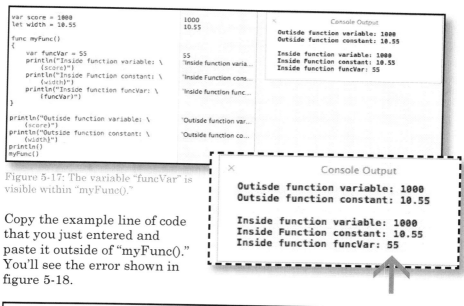

Figure 5-17: The variable "funcVar" is visible within "myFunc()."

Copy the example line of code that you just entered and paste it outside of "myFunc()." You'll see the error shown in figure 5-18.

```
Console Output

Outisde function variable: 1000
Outside function constant: 10.55

Inside function variable: 1000
Inside Function constant: 10.55
Inside function funcVar: 55
```

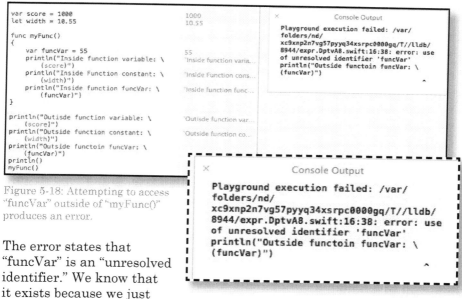

Figure 5-18: Attempting to access "funcVar" outside of "myFunc()" produces an error.

```
Console Output

Playground execution failed: /var/
folders/nd/
xc9xnp2n7vg57pyyq34xsrpc0000gq/T//lldb/
8944/expr.DptvA8.swift:16:38: error: use
of unresolved identifier 'funcVar'
println("Outside functoin funcVar: \
(funcVar)")
```

The error states that "funcVar" is an "unresolved identifier." We know that it exists because we just created it in "myFunc()," but the program can no longer access it. The unresolved identifier error occurred because when we created "funcVar" within a function, we created it with a **local** scope. Local scope variables are only visible and accessible within the function where they were declared.

local

In section three we used arguments in functions and we learned that the function treats the arguments as variables. We might expect arguments to be treated as locally scoped, then. To test the scope of function arguments, create a function called "twoNumbers" that takes two integer values as arguments and then prints them to the console. Your code should look like the following:

```
func twoNumbers(numA:Int,numb:Int)
{
    println("\(numA) \(numb)")
}
```

The example function is very simple. To test "twoNumbers()," call the function and pass it two valid arguments. Figure 5-19 shows you what you can expect your output to look like:

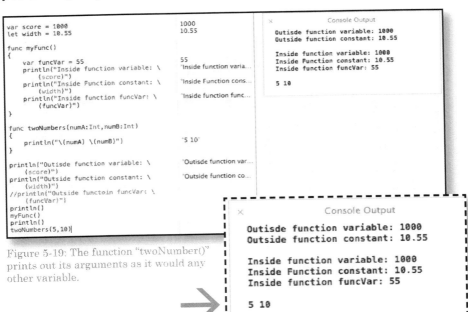

Figure 5-19: The function "twoNumber()" prints out its arguments as it would any other variable.

Once you've confirmed that "twoNumbers()" works, use the same println()
command outside of the function, below the function call.

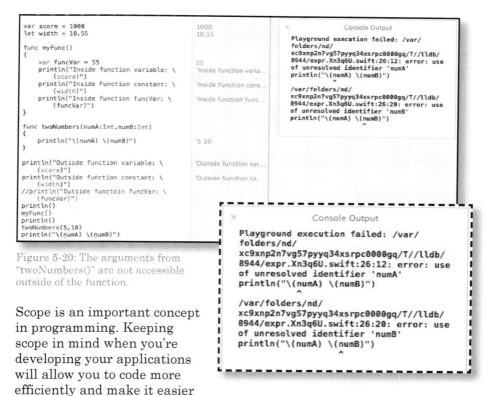

Figure 5-20: The arguments from
"twoNumbers()" are not accessible
outside of the function.

Scope is an important concept
in programming. Keeping
scope in mind when you're
developing your applications
will allow you to code more
efficiently and make it easier
to diagnose any bugs that come from improperly scoped elements.

In the final section of this chapter, we will look at nested functions.

QUESTIONS FOR REVIEW

1. In programming, scope refers to the visibility of a variable to other parts of the program.
   a. True.
   b. False.

2. How would you declare a variable with global scope?
   a. Using the "asGlobal" keyword.
   b. It would be declared within a special "globalVariables" array.
   c. It would be declared outside of any functions.
   d. It would be declared inside every function.

3. Which is true of a local variable?
   a. It can be used within the function that it is declared.
   b. It can be used within any function in the program.
   c. It must be specifically declared as local with a keyword.
   d. It is visible to the entire program.

4. Function arguments are local.
   a. True.
   b. False.

5.5 NESTED FUNCTIONS

Nested functions are functions that are declared inside the code block of other functions. Using nested functions we can declare a parent function and then, inside of that parent function, declare functions that contain encapsulated code that is specific to the parent function. We'll create a simple example below.

nested functions

In a fresh Xcode playground, enter the following code block:

```
func nested(i:Int,j:Int)
{
   func printAnswer(answer:Int)
   {
      // "printAnswer" function code
   }
   // "nested" function code
}
```

Nested inside main function.

In the preceding code example we declared a function, "nested()," that takes two parameters. Within "nested" we declared another function, "printAnswer()," that takes one parameter. As you can see, the syntax when declaring nested functions is the same as the syntax for declaring other functions.

Remove the commented out code from "nested()" and replace it with the following:

```
var sum = i + j
printAnswer(sum)
```

You'll notice while entering the preceding code that Xcode is aware of the "printAnswer()" function that you've declared. A code completion bubble will appear, as shown here in figure 5-21:

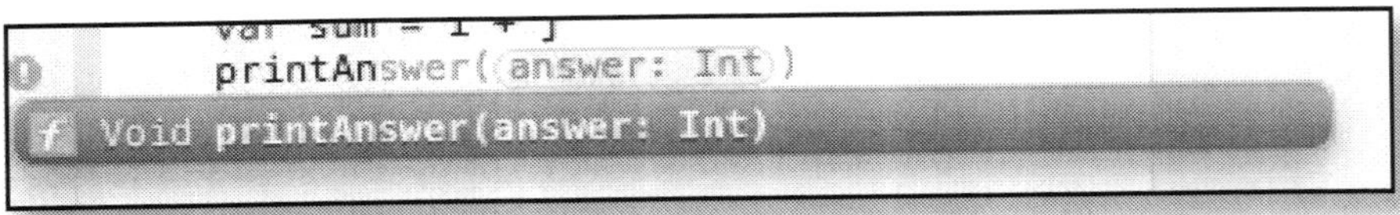

Figure 5-21: Xcode's code completion bubble suggests the nested function that was just declared.

The code for the parent function, "nested()," is complete. Replace the comments within "printAnswer()" with the following code:

```
println("\(answer)")
```

As you may have guessed, we are having "printAnswer()" output the value of our variable, "sum."

Your complete code should look like the following:

```
func nested(i:Int, j:Int)
{
    func printAnswer(answer:Int)
    {
        println("\(answer)")
    }
    var sum = i + j
    printAnswer(sum)
}
```

Notice the code indentation pattern we are using. Swift does not require indentation in order to compile, but Xcode has been automatically formatting certain code elements as you've been working. Formatting is done to improve readability for the programmer and is especially useful when dealing with nested functions and complex conditionals.

Now that the code is complete, call the parent function, "nested()," and pass it two integers.

```
nested(6,7)
```

The arguments will be passed to "nested()." Those arguments will be used in the variable declaration for the integer "sum" and "sum" will then be passed as an argument to the nested function "printAnswer()." Figure 5-22 shows you what your console output should look like:

```
func nested(i:Int,j:Int)
{
    func printAnswer(answer:Int)
    {
        println("\(answer)")          "13"
    }
    var sum = i + j                    13
    printAnswer(sum)
}
nested(6,7)|
```

```
×          Console Output
13
```

Figure 5-22: The nested function "printAnswer()" is called within "nested()" and outputs to the console.

Our example was very simple, but you can understand how being able to encapsulate frequently used code within a function will help you better organize your code and keep you from repeating code in your program.

1. A nested function can be called from anywhere in the program.
   a. True.
   b. False.

2. What do nested functions allow us to do? (Choose all that apply.)
   a. Better organize our code.
   b. Limit repeated code in our program.
   c. Make local variables visible to the entire program.
   d. Encapsulate code blocks within a function.

3. Code indentation is not considered by the Swift compiler.
   a. True.
   b. False.

4. Xcode's code completion bubble ignores nested functions.
   a. True.
   b. False.

CHAPTER 5 LAB EXERCISE

1) Open a new playground called SLA_Lab5. In the text editor, erase any unnecessary code and leave the necessary import statement.

2) Create a multiline comment that lists your name, the date, and the name of the lab assignment (SLA_Lab5).

3) Write a function that takes two arguments labeled rows and columns. The function should return a String. The string should contain a matrix made out of asterisk symbols with the correct number of rows and columns.

For example, if the values 7 and 3 are passed to the function, the function should return a String that looks like this:

```
***
***
***
***
***
***
***
```

> **Hint**: println() with no argument will produce a new line character if needed.

4) Test your function by making several calls to the function, passing it different values. You may notice that if you pass a very large number to the function you get a poor result.

5) Add code to your function to limit the number of rows and/or columns printed to 20.

6) Create another function that takes a single integer value and returns a Double value. Call the function inchesToFeet. Perform the conversion inside the function by dividing the value of the argument by 12 and returning that value.

7) Write a function call to test your function. Once your function is working correctly, try sending a Double value as an argument to the function. What is the result?

You've run into a limitation of functions: you can't use a single function for multiple argument types. You can also only return a singular type. At this point, you'd have to write and implement an entirely new function that accepts Doubles as arguments.

8) Rewrite the function so you can supply a Double as an argument. Note that you'll have to give the function a different name.

This problem is alleviated by Generics, which are covered later.

CHAPTER SUMMARY

In this chapter we introduced functions. Functions allow us to organize our code better and encapsulate frequently used code blocks in a structured manner. We learned that functions can take arguments and then process those arguments. Functions can also return values that we can use later in our program. We also gained an understanding of how variable scope works. Finally, we examined the use of nested functions to better organize our code.

In the next chapter we will learn about Classes and Protocols in Swift.

CHAPTER 6

CLASSES AND PROTOCOLS

CHAPTER OBJECTIVES:

- You will learn how enumerations can allow you to work with groups of related values in a type-safe way.
- You will learn what a class is and how classes are implemented in Swift.
- You will understand inheritance between classes and subclasses.
- You will use overrides in subclasses to implement different versions of class methods.
- You will learn about protocols and how to implement them with classes.

6.1 ENUMS

So far while programming in Swift we have been using the standard data types. In many circumstances, the standard data types will be all that you need, but there may be situations where you want to create your own specific type. Swift allows you to do this using enumerations.

An **enumeration**, or **enum**, is a defined common type that is used for a group of related values that can then be used in a type-safe way. **Type safety** in programming is the degree to which a language prevents type errors—the errors that occur when there is a discrepancy between an expected type and a provided type. The best way to understand enums is by working with them, so open up Xcode and set up a fresh playground.

> **enum**
>
> **type safety**

We're going to use the days of the week as the basis for our enum examples. We chose days of the week because they represent a limited set of similar data. Days of the week could be represented using Strings or Ints fairly easily, but both of those data types have a range that far exceeds what we would expect for days of the week. If we used integers to represent days of the week, there would be substantially more values available then the seven we would need to represent our data. It would be easy to mistakenly use a value, eight, for example, that would be out of range. Also, using an Int to represent days of the week will lead to more opaque code.

Using an enum for days of the week ensures that data is type safe, meaning that Xcode will generate an error if we attempt to use an invalid value.

Enter the following code to begin working with enums:

```
enum Day
{
    // enum definition will go here
}
```

You have created the shell of an enum with the preceding code. The keyword **enum** introduces the enumeration and the curly brackets contain the definition code block.

Within the "Day" enum code block, define the member values of the enumeration using the following code:

```
case Monday
case Tuesday
case Wednesday
case Thursday
case Friday
case Saturday
case Sunday
```

You can see that you use the "case" keyword to define an enumeration member. We have entered the proper name of every day of the week as the member values, meaning that if you declare a variable as the "Day" type it must hold the value Monday, Tuesday, Wednesday, Thursday, Friday, Saturday, or Sunday. The following code will declare a "Day" variable.

```
var firstDay = Day.Monday
```

Your Xcode playground should match figure 6-1.

Figure 6-1: Defining the enumeration "Day" and creating a variable of type "Day" named "firstDay."

Declaring a variable of an enum type is done in a similar manner to any other variable declaration. The var keyword is used, followed by the variable name and the assignment operator. The assigned value is in a different format then we've seen before. The name of the enum type is used with dot notation followed by one of the valid enum members. The enum assignment is informing the Swift compiler that you want the variable to be of type "Day" and of a specific "Day" value.

> **Tip:** The enumeration you've defined is a type, so you can also use the explicit type declaration syntax you're accustomed to. "var firstDay:Day = .Monday" is also a valid declaration.

Now that "firstDay" has been declared as type "Day" you can output it in the same way you would output any other variable. Use println() to output "firstDay" to the console and compare your output to figure 6-2.

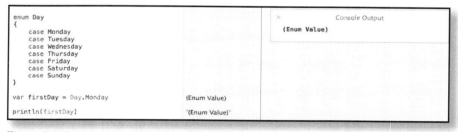

Figure 6-2: An enum type output produces "(Enum Value)" in the console output window.

In the output there isn't any specific value, only "(Enum Value)." You're getting that result because the compiler does not have an associated value for "Day.Monday" to output to the console. All it can output is the information that the value is an enumeration. In order to use enumeration members, you need to explicitly instruct your program what to do with them.

Before we continue, though, we're going to modify the value of "firstDay." Now that it is declared as type "Day" we no longer need to use the full dot notation to modify it, but we do need to ensure that any value we set it as is a valid member of "Day." Use the following code to change the value of "firstDay."

```
firstDay = .Tuesday
```

You've now assigned "firstDay" the value of the ".Tuesday" member of the enumeration "Day." Change it to the following code:

```
firstDay = .Lunes
```

You've used the correct syntax, but Xcode has an error, seen in figure 6-3.

```
enum Day                                          Console Output
{
    case Monday                          Playground execution failed: /var/
    case Tuesday                         folders/nd/
    case Wednesday                       xc9xnp2n7vg57pyyq34xsrpc0000gq/T//lldb/
    case Thursday                        8944/expr.4u0ylC.swift:16:13: error:
    case Friday                          'Day.Type' does not have a member named
    case Saturday                        'Lunes'
    case Sunday                          firstDay = .Lunes
}                                                   ^

var firstDay = Day.Monday      (Enum Value)

firstDay = .Lunes              (Enum Value)
```

Figure 6-3: Xcode encounters an error when attempting to assign an unknown enum member to a variable.

"Lunes" was never defined in "Day," so when we attempt to assign it to the "firstDay" variable Xcode gives us an error. That error shows how using enumerations is type safe. "Lunes" is not a value of type "Day," so we cannot use it as the value of a "Day" type variable. Change your code back so that "firstDay" has the value ".Tuesday."

We are going to use a switch statement to match our enumeration values. Below the "firstDay" declaration, enter the following code:

```
switch firstDay
{
case .Monday:
    println("Today is Monday")
case .Tuesday:
    println("Today is Tuesday")
default:
    println("Today is neither Monday nor
Tuesday")
}
```

The switch statement in the preceding code uses the members of the enumeration "Day" as its cases. We have only created specific cases for ".Monday" and ".Tuesday," - so we had to include the "default" statement because a switch statement, as you may remember from section 3.3 - must be comprehensive. After entering the example code, you should be looking at the output seen in figure 6-4.

```
enum Day                                                 ×          Console Output
{                                                        Today is Tuesday
    case Monday
    case Tuesday
    case Wednesday
    case Thursday
    case Friday
    case Saturday
    case Sunday
}

var firstDay = Day.Monday        (Enum Value)

firstDay = .Tuesday              (Enum Value)

switch firstDay
{
case .Monday:
    println("Today is Monday")
case .Tuesday:
    println("Today is Tuesday")      "Today is Tuesday"
default:
    println("Today is neither Monday nor
        Tuesday")
}
```

Figure 6-4: Using a switch statement to match enumeration values.

The console displays "Today is Tuesday" because the switch statement runs the code block in the ".Tuesday" case. If you change "firstDay" to another day of the week, the switch statement will match it appropriately.

In chapter five we learned about functions and function arguments. "Day" is now a type, so we can encapsulate our switch statement in a function that takes a variable of type "Day" as an argument. Declare a function according to the following code example and place your switch statement within its code block.

```
func dayCheck(day:Day)
{
    // Put your switch statement here
}
```

Notice that in the "dayCheck()" function we use an argument named "day" that is of type "Day," our enumeration type. Modify your switch statement to validate "day" as in the following code:

```
switch day
{
    // switch code block
}
```

Now, you can call the "dayCheck()" function with "firstDay" as a parameter. Make the following further changes to cover all of the members of "Day:"

```
func dayCheck(day:Day)
{
    // Declare a local variable to
    // hold the name of the day
    var dayVal:String
    switch day
    {
```

```
      case .Monday:
            dayVal = "Monday"
    case .Tuesday:
            dayVal = "Tuesday"
      case .Wednesday:
            dayVal = "Wednesday"
      case .Thursday:
            dayVal = "Thursday"
      case .Friday:
            dayVal = "Friday"
      case .Saturday:
            dayVal = "Saturday"
      case .Sunday:
            dayVal = "Sunday"
      }
      println("Today is \(dayVal)")
      }
}
```

The function declares a local variable named "dayVal" of type String
to hold the String value that we want to print. The switch statement
covers every member of enum "Day" and so does not require a "default"
statement. In the case code blocks, the value of "dayVal" is set according
to the enum's member values. After the switch statement completes, a
println() command uses the "dayVal" String in its console output. Try
calling our function with your "firstDay" variable, like the following code
sample:

```
dayCheck(firstDay)
```

Your console output should match figure 6-5.

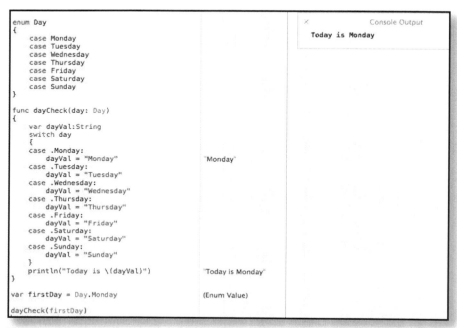

```
enum Day
{
    case Monday
    case Tuesday
    case Wednesday
    case Thursday
    case Friday
    case Saturday
    case Sunday
}

func dayCheck(day: Day)
{
    var dayVal:String
    switch day
    {
    case .Monday:
        dayVal = "Monday"                    "Monday"
    case .Tuesday:
        dayVal = "Tuesday"
    case .Wednesday:
        dayVal = "Wednesday"
    case .Thursday:
        dayVal = "Thursday"
    case .Friday:
        dayVal = "Friday"
    case .Saturday:
        dayVal = "Saturday"
    case .Sunday:
        dayVal = "Sunday"
    }
    println("Today is \(dayVal)")           "Today is Monday"
}

var firstDay = Day.Monday                    (Enum Value)

dayCheck(firstDay)
```

```
✕                    Console Output
Today is Monday
```

Figure 6-5: Functions can use enumerations as arguments.

Enumeration allows us to create type-safe groups of similar values and to work with them in a clear, efficient way. In the next section, we'll look at creating and instantiating classes in Swift.

QUESTIONS FOR REVIEW

1. Using enumeration is a type safe way to work with groups of similar data.
   a. True.
   b. False.

2. What is a proper enum declaration?
   a. enum myEnum { // member definition }
   b. func myEnum:enum { // member definition }
   c. var myEnum: enum = [// member definition]
   d. let enum myEnum = [// member definition]

3. What happens when you assign a variable of type enum the value of an undeclared member?
   a. A new enum member is defined.
   b. A default enum member is used.
   c. Xcode produces a type error.
   d. Nothing, it is ignored.

4. Which of the following would be a good candidate for enumeration?
   a. Months of the year.
   b. A list of technology companies.
   c. Planets in the solar system.
   d. All of the above.

6.2 CREATING A CLASS AND INSTANTIATION

In this section we're going to be looking at classes in Swift. A **class** is a code module designed to represent a real world object in your app. Classes are used as building blocks of an app.

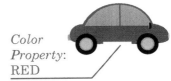

To illustrate the class concept, let's start with a theoretical example. In reality, you have a car that is a physical object. In code, to represent that car in a way that's meaningful for your program you would create a car class. Your real-life car can be described in certain ways: it is red, it has four doors, it has a top speed of 120MPH, and it was built in 2010. In your program, your car class will have properties that you will set: a color property, a style property, a speed property, and a model year property. In reality, your car can perform some actions: it can accelerate, decelerate, and turn. Your car class instead has methods that you will create: speedUp(), slowDown() and turn(). In real life you had to buy your car. In code, you have to instantiate your car class. Using a class, you create an abstract idea of an object that you can manipulate in your program.

Color Property:
RED

Let's create a real example. In a new Xcode playground we'll create a "Dog" class. Enter the following code block:

```
class Dog
{
    // Properties and Methods
}
```

This code is the basic class definition syntax. The keyword **class** followed by "Dog" creates a class named "Dog." The curly brackets define the code block that will contain the properties and methods for your class. Figure 6-6 shows the class outline in the Xcode editor.

```
class Dog
{
    // Properties and Methods
}
```
| | Console Output |

Figure 6-6: A class definition outline.

Now we need to consider what attributes of real dogs we're interested in abstracting for our app. For now, let's keep it simple and only concern ourselves with the dog's name, breed, and age. Erase the comment and enter the following code in its place:

```
// Properties
var Name:String
var Breed:String
var Age:Int
```

You likely noticed that we declared variables without assigning them any values and that your output console filled up with errors, shown in figure 6-7.

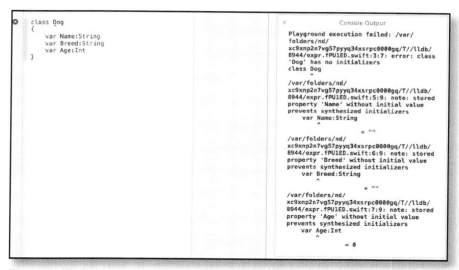

Figure 6-7: Xcode errors informing you that class properties have not been set.

The variables that we declared are the class' **properties**. Properties are a means to associate values to a particular class and represent the adjectives that would describe a real-world object. Properties in Swift classes can be stored or computed. In this section, we're working with stored properties, which store the values of constants or variables. We will touch on computed properties in chapter seven.

The properties are not assigned any values because each dog that we create, or **instantiate**, later will have a different name, breed, and age. Those instances' properties will store the values we eventually assign. You can consider our

Instantiate:
Represent as or by an instance.

"Dog" class to be the blueprint of a dog in code. It contains all of the attributes that we want a dog to have and it defines all of the actions that we want a dog to take, but it does not yet refer to an individual dog. We create the property names as proper nouns and start them with a capital letter.

The error messages seen in figure 6-7 are informing us that there is currently no way to assign values to the properties that we have created. We could have assigned all of the properties default values, but instead we will create an initializer function. Enter the following code inside your class code block and below your properties:

```
// Initializer
init(name:String, breed:String, age:Int)
{
    Name = name
    Breed = breed
    Age = age
}
```

You should no longer have any errors and your Xcode playground should look like figure 6-8.

```
class Dog
{
    var Name:String
    var Breed:String
    var Age:Int

    // Initialiser
    init(name:String, breed:String,
        age:Int)
    {
        Name = name
        Breed = breed
        Age = age
    }
}
```

Console Output

Figure 6-8: Setting up an initializer resolves the Xcode errors.

An **initializer** is a special type of class method that is defined with the **init** keyword and is run every time a class is instantiated. It initializes the properties of a class and establishes the arguments that need to be passed when you instantiate the class in your code.

init

In the preceding example case you can see that the initializer is a special type of function. In the parentheses we define the argument names and the data type we expect. Whenever we create a "Dog" class we need to know the dog's name, its breed, and its age. Note that the argument names are the same as our property names but they are all lowercase. When we assign values in the body of the initializer we are assigning the properties, "Name," "Breed," and "Age," the values that were passed as arguments, "name," "breed," and "age."

Below the initializer (but still within the class's code block) we will enter the actions that we want our dogs to be able to do. In our case, that will be to bark, sit, and run. Enter the following code:

```
// Methods
func sit()
{
    println("\(Name) is sitting")
}
func bark()
{
    println("\(Name) is barking. Woof
woof!")
}
func run()
{
    println("\(Name) is running!")
}
```

All of the preceding code is familiar to you from our work on functions in chapter five, but functions within a class are called **methods** and are associated with the class. Our "bark()" method gets the "Name" variable from the class and outputs a String to the console, for example.

```
class Dog
{
    // Properties
    var Name:String
    var Breed:String
    var Age:Int

    // Initialiser
    init(name:String, breed:String,
        age:Int)
    {
        Name = name
        Breed = breed
        Age = age
    }

    // Methods
    func sit()
    {
        println("\(Name) is sitting")
    }
    func bark()
    {
        println("\(Name) is barking. Woof
            woof!")
    }
    func run()
    {
        println("\(Name) is running!")
    }
}
```

	Console Output

Figure 6-9: Our "Dog" class with methods included. Note that even though we call println() in the methods, nothing is output to the console yet.

We could use the class as it is, but we're going to add a few methods that will return the values of our class properties. We can refer to class properties directly using dot notation, but it is safer to access them through class methods. We will call these methods "getAge()," "getBreed()," and "getName()." All of these methods will return a value. Enter the following code under the methods we've already built:

```
func getAge()->Int
{
    return Age
}
func getBreed()->String
{
    return Breed
}
func getName()->String
{
    return Name
}
```

As you can see, the methods we've just created return the appropriate data type for the property that they refer to. Figure 6-10 shows you what your completed "Dog" class should look like.

```
class Dog
{
    // Properties
    var Name:String
    var Breed:String
    var Age:Int

    // Initialiser
    init(name:String, breed:String,
        age:Int)
    {
        Name = name
        Breed = breed
        Age = age
    }

    // Methods
    func sit()
    {
        println("\(Name) is sitting")
    }
    func bark()
    {
        println("\(Name) is barking. Woof
            woof!")
    }
    func run()
    {
        println("\(Name) is running!")
    }


    func getAge()->Int
    {
        return Age
    }
    func getBreed()->String
    {
        return Breed
    }
    func getName()->String
    {
        return Name
    }
}
```

Figure 6-10: The completed "Dog" class, ready to be instantiated.

In order to actually use the class that we've created, we have to instantiate it. Instantiation is the creation of an individual dog with its own unique properties and methods. We are creating an instance of the "Dog" class that has specific properties that we will define.

Outside of the "Dog" class definition enter the following code:

```
let aDog = Dog(name:"Rover",
breed:"Collie", age:8)
let bDog = Dog(name:"Freddie", breed:"Lab",
age:4)
```

We have just created two instances of the "Dog" class. As you entered the previous example code, an Xcode code completion bubble will have appeared, as shown in figure 6-11:

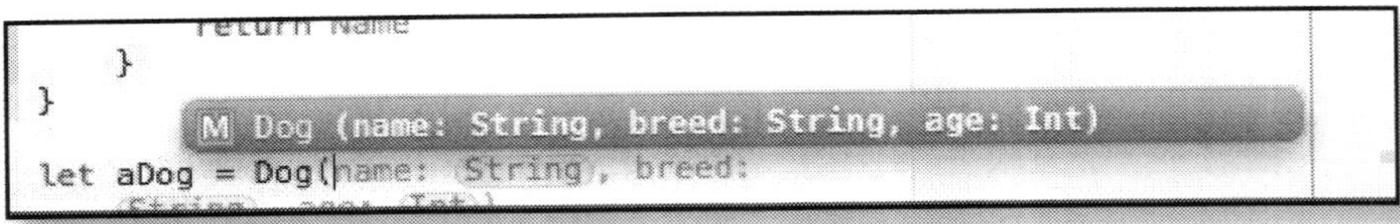

Figure 6-11: Xcode shows us what information is needed in order to instantiate our "Dog" class.

The code completion bubble is informing us that our "Dog" class needs a name that is a String, a breed that is a String, and an age that is an Int. In the code you can see the correct syntax for class instantiation. Also note that you need to include keywords for the initializer.

Now that we have instantiated two dogs we can make them execute some action. Below the class instantiations, enter the following code:

```
aDog.bark()
aDog.run()
bDog.sit()
```

We are using dot notation to access the methods in the "Dog" class in the instances we've created. Look at the console output and you'll see that the methods have been executed and the String interpolation we used in the println() commands accessed the correct properties for "aDog" and "bDog."

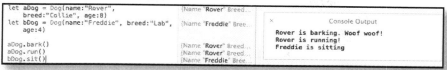

Figure 6-12: The result of calling the "bark()," "sit()," and "run()" methods from the "Dog" class.

Enter the following code to test our "get" methods and ensure that the class is correctly returning data.

```
Console Output

Rover is barking. Woof woof!
Rover is running!
Freddie is sitting
```

```
println(aDog.getBreed())
println(bDog.getBreed())
println(aDog.getAge())
```

Compare your output to figure 6-13. You can see that calling class methods that return data is just as easy as calling functions that return data because methods are functions.

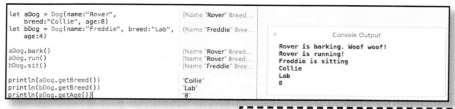

Figure 6-13: Class methods return data in the same manner as functions.

Classes allow you to create abstract representations of real world objects to use in your code. Abstraction and compartmentalization allow you to create modular programs are the

```
Console Output

Rover is barking. Woof woof!
Rover is running!
Freddie is sitting
Collie
Lab
8
```

core of object-oriented programming. In the next section we'll delve into using subclasses and overriding methods.

1. What do classes allow you to do in your program?
   a. Organize groups of similar data in a type-safe manner.
   b. Create abstract representations of real-world objects.
   c. List information according to key-value pairs.
   d. Remove unused information from memory.

2. Which of the following is a proper class declaration?
   a. let myClass:class = { // class code block }
   b. class myClass = { // class code block }
   c. class myClass { // class code block }
   d. class myClass() { // class code block}

3. What does init() do within a class?
   a. Initializes properties when the class is instantiated.
   b. Initializes properties when the class is declared.
   c. Resets all of the class properties to their default values.
   d. Nothing, it is only there for readability.

4. Functions that are declared within classes are known as "methods."
   a. True.
   b. False.

6.3 SUBCLASSES AND OVERRIDES

In the previous section we introduced the idea of classes and at the end of the section we mentioned **Object-Oriented Programming (OOP)**. In coding, instances of a class are traditionally known as **objects**. Object-oriented programming is the use of objects and their methods and properties as the foundation of a program. Due to the underlying nature of Swift classes, you will often find that Swift's official documentation refers to objects with the more general term **instance**. The differences between Swift classes and traditional classes are beyond the scope of this book, but you can go to the Apple developer library to explore the official documentation.

OOP

Object-Oriented Programming

In order for OOP to be most effective there has to be a hierarchy of classes with collections of well-defined, complimentary objects. Defining hierarchy is done in Swift using **subclasses**. Subclasses are hierarchical children of a parent class and share key properties and methods with that parent class, but they are specific enough to warrant being a class themselves. The subclass concept is most easily understood through examples.

objects

instance

subclass

In the beginning of section 6.2 we used a car as an example of an object. We will build on that example here.

A "Car" class is clear and well defined, but if your application is solving a problem that involves many types of vehicles, you might have "Car" properties and methods that overlap with other class' properties and methods. As an example, consider a truck. A truck is unique enough that we would define it differently from a car, however, it is easy to imagine methods and properties that would overlap both a "Car" class and a "Truck" class. It would make sense to define a broader class, "Vehicle," that contains the methods and properties that we know must be a part of both "Car" and "Truck."

The broader "Vehicle" class is a parent class, and the more specific "Car" and "Truck" classes are child classes. The child class is said to *inherit* the methods and properties of its parent. If "Vehicle" has a "Speed" property, then both "Car" and "Truck" will have a "Speed" property. Parent classes do not inherit from their children, and sibling classes do not inherit from each other. If "Truck" has an "IsPickup" Boolean then that property would be unique to "Truck" and would not be a property of either "Vehicle" or "Car."

We can see that the classes "Vehicle," "Car," and "Truck" are all well defined and complimentary. Parent classes are always more generic and child classes are always more specific. Open an Xcode playground and enter the following code to begin working with parent and child classes.

```
class Vehicle
{
    var MaxSpeed:Double
    var CurrentSpeed = 0.0
    var Make:String
}
```

The preceding code creates a class named "Vehicle" and defines that class as having the properties "MaxSpeed," "CurrentSpeed," and "Make." You'll notice that "MaxSpeed" and "Make" are defined the same way the properties of "Dog" from section 6.2 were, but that "CurrentSpeed" is assigned a value. Your console output will give you some errors, as shown in figure 6-14.

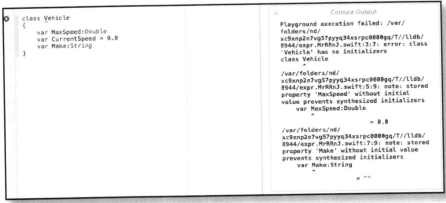

Figure 6-14: Xcode gives errors for "MaxSpeed" and "Make," but not "CurrentSpeed."

The errors are informing us that there are no initializers for "MaxSpeed" or "Make," but Xcode is not giving an error for "CurrentSpeed" because we have assigned "CurrentSpeed" a default value. We do not need to initialize the value of "CurrentSpeed" in an initializer, as it will always be assigned 0.0 for any "Vehicle" object we create.

To resolve those errors, create the following initializer in your "Vehicle" class:

```
init (maxSpeed:Double, make:String)
{
    MaxSpeed = maxSpeed
    Make = make
}
```

```
class Vehicle
{
    var MaxSpeed:Double
    var CurrentSpeed = 0.0
    var Make:String

    init (maxSpeed:Double, make:String)
    {
        MaxSpeed = maxSpeed
        Make = make
    }
}
```

Console Output

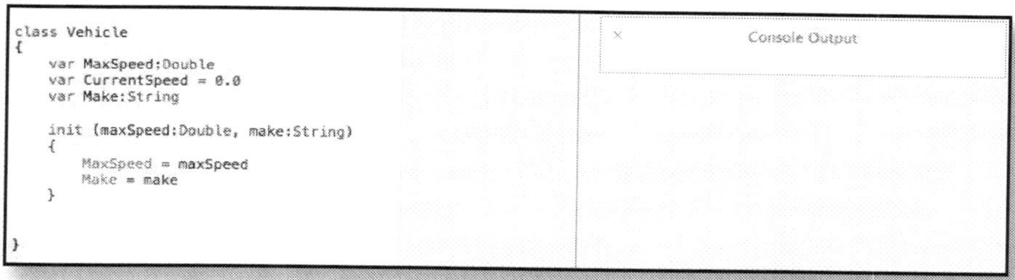

Figure 6-15: After including the initializer, Xcode's errors are resolved.

We now have a valid "Vehicle" class with properties, but before we continue we'll add a few methods to "Vehicle." Create two methods that return the "MaxSpeed" and "Make" properties called "getSpeed()" and "getMake()."

```
func getSpeed()->Double
{
    return MaxSpeed
}
func getMake()->String
{
    return Make
}
```

Those methods will exist for any subclasses of "Vehicle," allowing any vehicle type we choose to represent in code to return its speed and make. We can be confident about the implementation of "getSpeed()"

and "getMake()" across all vehicles because we know they will have "MaxSpeed" and "Make" properties. But what do we do for methods that we know every subclass will contain, but that we also know will be implemented differently for each subclass? Enter the following code below the methods you implemented in the preceding code:

```
func makeNoise()
{

}
```

You can see that "makeNoise()" is a valid method, but it doesn't actually do anything. The reason is because we know that different vehicles will make noise differently, so when we create a subclass it will implement its own specific version of "makeNoise()." Outside of the "Vehicle" class definition, enter the following code to create a subclass:

```
class Car:Vehicle
{
    override func makeNoise()
    {
        // "Car" specific "makeNoise()" code
goes here
    }
}
```

While you were entering the preceding code, Xcode will have offered a code completion bubble as you can see here in figure 6-16:

```
class Vehicle
{
    var MaxSpeed:Double
    var CurrentSpeed = 0.0
    var Make:String

    init (maxSpeed:Double, make:String)
    {
        MaxSpeed = maxSpeed
        Make = make
    }

    func getSpeed()->Double
    {
        return MaxSpeed
    }
    func getMake()->String
    {
        return Make
    }

    func makeNoise()
    {
    }
}
class Car:Vehicle
{
    makeNoise()
```

Figure 6-16: Your complete "Vehicle" class with an Xcode code completion bubble informing you that the "makeNoise()" function is available to be overridden.

First, the preceding code contains a class definition for "Car" followed by a colon and the name of the parent class, "Vehicle." We are saying, "create a class Car that inherits from class Vehicle." "Car" is a subclass of "Vehicle" and will have all of the properties and methods of "Vehicle."

<code>class Car:Vehicle</code>

Within the "Car" definition we find another "makeNoise()" method, but it is preceded by the "override" keyword. An **override** is a subclass method that modifies the method from its parent class. In our example case, "makeNoise()" within "Car" is different from "makeNoise()" in "Vehicle." If a "Car" object calls the "makeNoise()" method, it will be called from "Car" and not from "Vehicle."

override

Complete your subclass definitions using the code that follows, and then we will see the override in practice:

```
class Car:Vehicle
{
    override func makeNoise()
    {
        println("Honk")
    }
    func accelerate()
    {
        println("Accelerating!")
    }
}
class Ambulance:Vehicle
{
    override func makeNoise()
    {
        println("WAAAAAHHHHH!")
    }
}
```

Here we have our complete "Car" subclass and we've created an
"Ambulance" subclass as well. Figure 6-17 shows how the definitions
should look in Xcode.

```swift
class Vehicle
{
    var MaxSpeed:Double
    var CurrentSpeed = 0.0
    var Make:String

    init (maxSpeed:Double, make:String)
    {
        MaxSpeed = maxSpeed
        Make = make
    }

    func getSpeed()->Double
    {
        return MaxSpeed
    }
    func getMake()->String
    {
        return Make
    }

    func makeNoise()
    {
    }
}
class Car:Vehicle
{
    override func makeNoise() {
        println("Honk")
    }
    func accelerate()
    {
        println("Accelerating!")
    }
}
class Ambulance:Vehicle
{
    override func makeNoise() {
        println("WAAAAAAHHHHHH!")
    }
}
```

Figure 6-17: The "Vehicle" parent class and the "Car" and "Ambulance" subclasses.

We can now create objects of these class types. Enter the following code:

```
let aCar = Car(maxSpeed:75, make:"Jeep")
let anAmbu = Ambulance(maxSpeed:105,
make:"Ambulance Company")
```

You can see that the object instantiation of a subclass is identical to the instantiation of a class. Note that the gutter includes the properties that we have assigned when we instantiated the objects, as seen in figure 6-18.

```
let aCar = Car(maxSpeed:75, make:"Jeep")          {{MaxSpeed 75.0 Cur...
let anAmbu = Ambulance(maxSpeed:105,              {{MaxSpeed 105.0 C...
    make:"Ambulance Company")
```

Figure 6-18: The syntax for creating an object of a subclass is identical to creating an object of a class. The gutter displays the object's property values.

We now have a "Vehicle" class, "Car" and "Ambulance" subclasses, and two instantiated objects—one of class "Car" and one of class "Ambulance." Use the following method calls to make our objects do something.

```
aCar.makeNoise()
anAmbu.makeNoise()
```

Your console output should match what you see in figure 6-19:

```
let aCar = Car(maxSpeed:75, make:"Jeep")      {{MaxSpeed 75.0 Cur...    ✕        Console Output
let anAmbu = Ambulance(maxSpeed:105,          {{MaxSpeed 105.0 C...
    make:"Ambulance Company")                                          Honk
                                                                       WAAAAAAHHHHHH!
aCar.makeNoise()                              {{MaxSpeed 75.0 Cur...
anAmbu.makeNoise()                            {{MaxSpeed 105.0 C...
```

Figure 6-19: Different subclasses have different outputs for the same method call because of overrides.

As you can see, calling the same "Vehicle" method from two different subclasses results in different outputs because those subclasses each used an override on the parent class' method. Ambulances and cars make different noises, but can both make noise, so our abstracted versions can both "makeNoise" but use different implementations.

Class hierarchies in OOP allow us to create better organized, more structured, and easier to implement program architectures. Using well-defined but complimentary classes allows you to tackle larger and more complicated programs.

In the final section of this chapter we will look into the Swift implementation of Protocols.

 QUESTIONS FOR REVIEW

1. It is often useful to have subclasses that are completely unrelated to their parent class.
   a. True.
   b. False.

2. What is the proper syntax to define a subclass?
   a. subclass mySubclass { // subclass code block }
   b. subclass mySubclass:myClass { // subclass code block }
   c. class mySubclass:myClass { // subclass code block }
   d. class mySubclass inherits myClass { // subclass code block }

3. An override allows a subclass to implement a different version of its parent class' method.
   a. True.
   b. False.

4. What is one benefit of object-oriented programming?
   a. Better organization and structure in large programs.
   b. An impressive title.
   c. The ability to organize functions by enumerations and implement subclassed constant variables.
   d. There are no benefits.

6.4 PROTOCOLS

Protocols in Swift (known as *interfaces* in some other programming languages) are program elements that define certain properties and methods that must be present in classes that utilize that protocol.

protocol

To better understand protocols we're going to consider an example outside of coding. Consider a home entertainment center. A normal home entertainment center will have a TV and it will probably have a DVD player, a video game console or two, and a cable box. The TV is the most important piece of the home entertainment puzzle because everything has to connect to the TV. The way that the other devices connect to the TV is through a standard cable, the HDMI cable. Each device that plugs into the TV, no matter who manufactured it, has to use the same type of HDMI cable and has to send the same type of information in the same manner. A game console is going to create an image in a different way than a DVD player, and a cable box is going to be different from either of them, but ultimately they all have to send the same type of image through the same type of cable.

That idea encapsulates the concept of protocols. For illustrative purposes, imagine that each device in the home entertainment center is a class. The purpose of the TV class is to handle output, and its methods expect specific arguments. The other classes—DVD player, game console and cable box—all want to interact with the TV class, but they've all been coded by different programmers to do different things and they generate output values in different ways. In order to ensure that every one of those classes, or any future classes, can interact with the TV class properly, they enforce the HDMI protocol. The HDMI protocol demands that any HDMI-compliant class will have certain properties and methods, thereby facilitating interaction between the TV class and the other classes.

Practically, using protocols allows you to further reduce instances of repeated code and, importantly, makes it easier for groups of programmers to work on large projects. While projects of that scale are beyond the scope of this book, it is useful to understand what protocols can do for you and how to implement them.

In order to show how protocols work, we'll use a simple example. In your Xcode playground, enter the following code:

```
protocol Travel
{
    func move()
}
```

In the preceding code block, we created a protocol named "Travel" using the **protocol** keyword. We're going to use the "Travel" protocol with any classes that we want to be able to travel. Classes that can travel have to move, so the "Travel" protocol enforces a method "move()" within any classes that implement it.

When we defined the "Travel" protocol and the "move()" method we did not include any implementation of "move()." All a protocol does is determine what methods or properties are required, it does not actually implement any of those methods or properties.

Create a class by entering the following code:

```
class Person:Travel
{
    // Code will go here
}
```

The class definition looks as though we are creating "Person" as a subclass of "Travel," but that's not what's happening here. Because "Travel" is a protocol, we are actually creating a class "Person" that implements the protocol "Travel." Notice that Xcode has come up with an error from the preceding code, as you can see in figure 6-20.

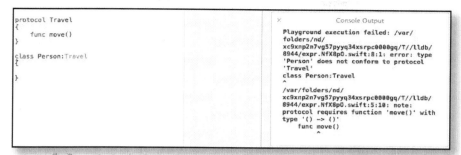

Figure 6-20: Xcode produces an error because "Person" has not yet implemented the methods required by the protocol "Travel."

The reason for the preceding error is that Xcode knows that any class that implements "Travel" must have a "move()" method and that "Person" does not have "move()" implemented yet. Include the following code in your "Person" class.

```
func move()
{
    println("Person is walking")
}
```

You'll see that the code you've just entered has resolved the Xcode error. The method "move()" is now implemented, so the requirements of the "Travel" protocol have been met.

Figure 6-21: Once the required methods are included, Xcode no longer shows an error for the "Person" class.

To demonstrate how we can use different implementations of the same protocol requirements, create a "Bird" class using the following code:

```
class Bird:Travel
{
    func move()
    {
        println("Bird is flying")
    }
}
```

In order to actually call those methods, create "Person" and "Bird" objects and then call "move()."

```
let aPerson = Person()
aPerson.move()
let aBird = Bird()
aBird.move()
```

You'll see from the console output, shown in figure 6-22, that while "Person" and "Bird" both implement the required "move()" method differently, they both meet the requirements of the "Travel" protocol.

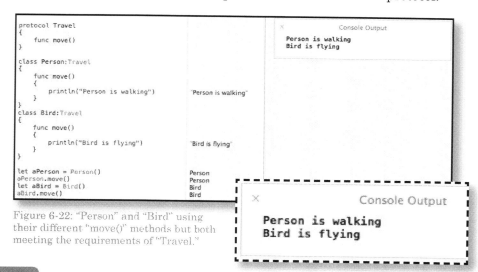

Figure 6-22: "Person" and "Bird" using their different "move()" methods but both meeting the requirements of "Travel."

We have only scratched the surface of protocols and their utility in object-oriented programming. As your skills develop and you build larger and more complex applications, you will find that protocols are an invaluable asset.

QUESTIONS FOR REVIEW

1. Does a protocol definition require method implementation?
   a. Yes.
   b. No.

2. Protocols have to be implemented with classes within the same hierarchy.
   a. True.
   b. False.

3. How does Xcode react to a class with a protocol implemented that does not yet have its requirements met?
   a. Xcode will create a skeleton for all of the required protocol elements.
   b. Xcode will generate an error.
   c. Xcode will ignore the unimplemented protocol requirements.
   d. Xcode will ignore the entire class.

4. Protocols determine the specifics of how their requirements are implemented in a given class.
   a. True.
   b. False.

CHAPTER 6 LAB EXERCISE

1) Open a new playground called SLA_Lab6. In the text editor, erase any unnecessary code and leave the necessary import statement.

2) Create a multiline comment that lists your name, the date, and the name of the lab assignment (SLA_Lab6).

3) Create a class called BankAccount. This class will represent an account at a bank. Think about the type of information that would need to be tracked for a bank account. What activities might a bank account class need to track?

4) Set up your BankAccount class according to the following:

Properties:
AccountID (Integer)
AccountHolderName (String)
Balance (Double)

Methods:
Debit (Takes Double as Argument / Returns Double (New Balance))
Credit (Takes Double As Argument / Returns Double (New Balance))
CheckBalance (Returns Double)

Don't forget to create your initializer.

5) Instantiate your Class with the following Instance:

```
MikesAccount
AccountID = 987654
AccountHolderName = "Mike Smith"
Balance = 500.00
```

6) Use your Debit() function to allow Mike to withdraw $100.00 from his account. Make sure the new balance of 400.00 is displayed.

7) Mike received his paycheck. Use the Credit() function to add $655.75 to his account balance and make sure the correct new balance is displayed.

8) Create a child class of BankAccount called checkingAccount. Remember that checkingAccount will inherit all of the properties and methods of its parent class. Add a method to checkingAccount called writeCheck().

writeCheck() will take three arguments:

checkNum   Integer
checkPayee   String
checkAmount   Double

Create the method so that the checkAmount is deducted from the balance and the information is displayed like this:

```
207             Joe's Cleaners        $25.00
New Balance: $450.55
```

9) Create an instance of the checkingAccount called MarysAccount with the following information:

```
AccountID = 456789
AccountHolderName = "Mary Sullivan"
Balance = 750.00
```

10) With the following arguments, use the write check method twice:

```
writeCheck(701, "Joes Cleaners", 25.00)
writeCheck(702, "Grocery King", $108.97)
```

Ensure the results are as expected. Debug your code if necessary.

CHAPTER SUMMARY

In this chapter we have gone over the basic concepts of object-oriented programming and learned about enumerations, classes, subclasses, and protocols. We have learned that enumerations allow us to create type-safe groups of related values. We saw that classes are a means of abstracting real-world objects into code concepts that we can instantiate as unique objects. We also learned about the parent/child inheritance between classes and subclasses and discussed creating well-defined, complimentary classes and subclasses. Finally, we touched on protocols with a theoretical example to demonstrate their utility and a practical example to learn the basic protocol syntax.

In the next chapter, we'll look at some of the extra goodies that you will find in the Swift language that will help make your development experience easier and more fun.

CHAPTER 7

MORE SWIFT GOODNESS

CHAPTER OBJECTIVES:

- You will learn how to use extensions to increase the utility of classes and data types.
- You will understand what operator overloading is and how it can be a powerful tool.
- You will utilize generic functions and learn how generics can result in less code repetition and better readability.
- You will see how Swift can use emoji.

7.1 EXTENSIONS

Until now, we have either used elements that are already built into the Swift language or we have created our own constructs. For example, each time we created an integer variable we have used the built in Int type. With our own constructs—the classes, prototypes and enums we've worked on—we have been able to add the exact functionality that we have needed. There will be times in development, though, when we will not be able to directly modify original code, or where we might want to have the built-in elements do more than they were designed for.

When increasing the functionality of an already existing code fragment, we could say that we are extending its utility beyond its design. That is exactly what **extensions** are in Swift: instance methods that are added to existing classes, structures or enums.

To demonstrate extensions, we will extend one of the basic data types to increase its functionality. In a new Xcode playground, enter the following:

```
extension Double
{
    // Extension code body goes here
}
```

In the example code we have used a new keyword, **extension**, to create an instanced method that we are adding to the Double class. We call it an instanced method because it only exists in the program where we declare it. We cannot permanently change the Double class.

Within our extension we're going to declare a few new properties of Doubles using a technique that we haven't discussed yet. We are going to use **computed properties** to get the values of these variables. Computed properties do not store a value but instead return the result of a calculation. The code to set and retrieve the values of computed properties are called *getters* and *setters*. In our example, we are going to use a *read-only computed property*. Read-only computed properties are only intended to be accessed, not set, and so only have a getter code block. A full explanation of computed properties is beyond the scope of this book, but documentation can be found at the Apple Developer site.

> **extension**

> **computed properties**

In the Double extension shell that you have just created, remove the comments and enter the following code:

```
var toFahrenheit : Double { return self *
9/5 + 32 }
var toCelsius : Double { return self - 32 *
5/9 }
```

The preceding code example has a number of familiar elements but also introduces new ideas. We understand that a property is being declared and that it's being assigned a name and an explicit type. Instead of a value, though, we have written a return statement and a code block. That code block is the getter code that calculates the value of the computed property.

The code example will assign the property "toFahrenheit" the value that is returned by the expression in the code block. The keyword **self** is referring to the value of the Double that called the "toFahrenheit" property and it is being used in the expression to calculate what its temperature is on the Fahrenheit scale. We then use the same syntax to determine what a given Fahrenheit temperature would be in Celsius.

> **self**

```
extension Double
{
    var toFahrenheit : Double { return self
        * 9/5 + 32}
    var toCelsius : Double { return self -
        32 * 5/9 }
}
```

Console Output

Figure 7-1: Extending the Double data type using computed properties.

Now that we have the extensions written, let's access them to make sure that they work properly. We'll begin with a known value, zero degrees Celsius. Enter the following code after your extension:

```
let temp:double_t = 0

println("\(temp) Degrees C is \(temp.
toFahrenheit) Degrees F")
```

We have created a constant Double and then used string interpolation to print the value of that Double and the computed property that we just extended the Double data type with, Double.toFahrenheit(). Your console output should match figure 7-2.

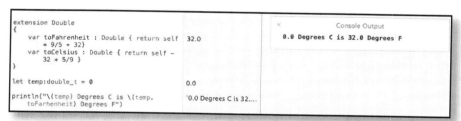

Figure 7-2: Our computed property returns the appropriate result when called.

Change the value of "temp" to 30 and check your console output against figure 7-3.

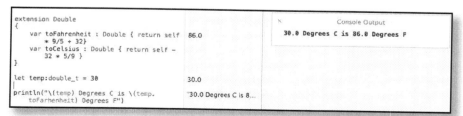

Figure 7-3: Verifying the implementation of the computed property.

Change the value of "temp" to 212, and then modify your code to convert that value to Celsius. Your resulting code should look like this:

```
println("\(temp) Degrees F is \(temp.
toCelsius) Degrees C")
```

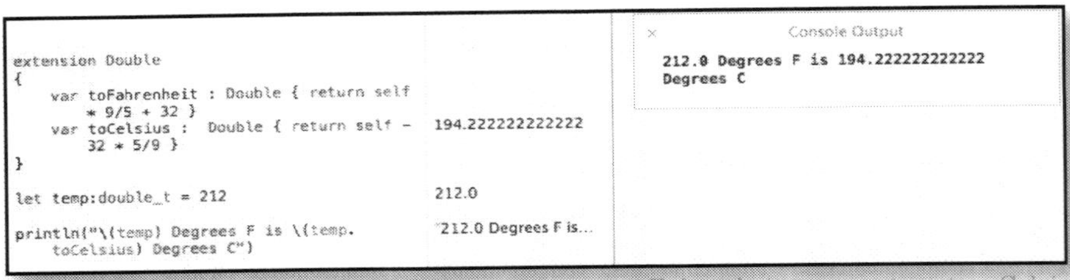

```
extension Double
{
    var toFahrenheit : Double { return self
        * 9/5 + 32 }
    var toCelsius :  Double { return self -     194.222222222222
        32 * 5/9 }
}

let temp:double_t = 212                         212.0

println("\(temp) Degrees F is \(temp.           "212.0 Degrees F is...
    toCelsius) Degrees C")
```

Console Output

**212.0 Degrees F is 194.222222222222
Degrees C**

Figure 7-4: Using an extension to Double to convert a Fahrenheit temperature to a Celsius temperature.

As you can see in the preceding code, extensions allow us to implement specific new methods and properties in established data types and classes within our projects. In the next section we'll look into a similar technique to add additional functionality to operators.

QUESTIONS FOR REVIEW

1. What is an extension?
   a. A means of adding functionality to existing code elements.
   b. A way to increase the precision of Floats or Doubles.
   c. Allowing a function extra time to return a value.
   d. A method of modifying an already existing class.

2. What is the proper syntax for an extension?
   a. func:extension Double
   b. extension Double
   c. extension T:Double
   d. extension (Double)

3. An extension will modify the original code for the element it's extending.
   a. True.
   b. False.

4. What does a computed property allow us to do?
   a. Use a pre-defined, default value.
   b. Use a passed in value.
   c. Assign a value according to the evaluation of a code block.
   d. None of the above.

7.2 OPERATOR OVERLOADING

In the previous section we looked at using extensions to add functionality to already existing classes or data types. In this section we'll examine how to achieve a similar result with operators using **operator overloading**. Operator overloading is a technique to add functionality to operators, making them more powerful, especially when working with user-generated enums, classes, and structures.

We've briefly mentioned **structures** before. Structures in Swift are primarily used to encapsulate a small set of simple values. They are similar to classes in that they can contain properties and methods. In the code that follows we will create a structure intended to store the data points needed to create a three dimensional vector, then we will create two vectors, and finally we will attempt to add them together using the standard addition operator. Defining a three dimensional vector requires three coordinates, referred to as x, y, and z, and adding two vectors is done by adding their respective x, y, and z coordinates together. Start a new Xcode playground and type in this code:

> **operator overloading**
>
> **structure**

```
struct Vector
{
    var x = 0
    var y = 0
    var z = 0
}

var v1 = Vector(x:5, y:8, z:5)
var v2 = Vector(x:9, y:4, z:2)

println(v1+v2)
```

The preceding code uses the **struct** keyword to create a structure. The syntax within the structure definition is similar to what we have seen with classes. The definitions of the three properties that will define a vector are made using the "var" keyword and they are all assigned an initial value, so no initializer is needed.

> **struct**

After the structure definition we create two variables of type "Vector" and assign the "Vector" properties that we have defined. Then, we attempt to print the result of adding the two vectors. Figure 7-5 shows the results of the example code.

```
struct Vector
{
    var x = 0
    var y = 0
    var z = 0
}

var v1 = Vector(x:5, y:8, z:5)      (x 5, y 8, z 5)
var v2 = Vector(x:9, y:4, z:2)      (x 9, y 4, z 2)

println(v1+v2)
```

```
×              Console Output

Playground execution failed: /var/
folders/nd/
xc9xnp2n7vg57pyyq34xsrpc8000gq/T//lldb/
8944/expr.YweYa8.swift:13:9: error:
'Vector' is not convertible to 'UInt8'
println(v1+v2)
          ^
```

Figure 7-5: The standard addition operator will not be able to add our "Vector" structures together.

The error generated from the preceding code informs us that Swift is unable to add two of our "Vector" structures together. In order to add "Vector" addition functionality we will overload the addition operator. Enter the following code into your playground, after your structure definition:

```
func + (augend: Vector, addend: Vector) ->
Vector
{
    return Vector(x: augend.x + addend.x,
y: augend.y + addend.y, z: augend.z +
addend.z)
}
```

You used the "func" keyword followed by the operator you want to overload. You then defined the arguments that you are going to pass to the overload (two of the "Vector" structures that we've defined) and finally you instructed the overload to return a value of type "Vector." Within the code block you have instructed Swift what the return "Vector" value is. In our example case, you have set the x, y, and z values of the return "Vector" as the sum of the input "Vector" x values, the sum of the input "Vector" y values, and the sum of the input "Vector" z values. Your code should now look like figure 7-6.

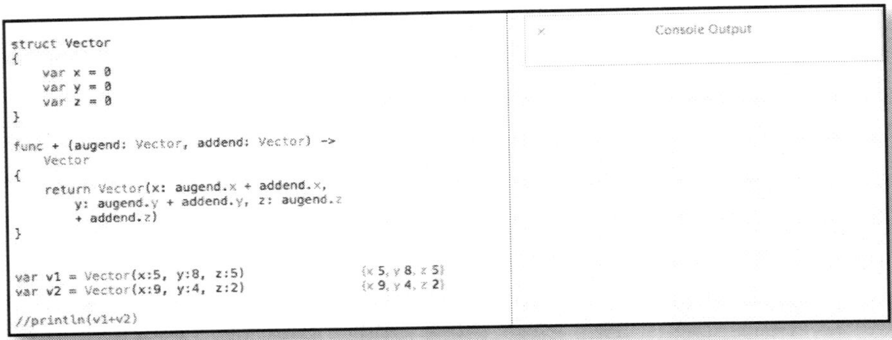

```
struct Vector
{
    var x = 0
    var y = 0
    var z = 0
}

func + (augend: Vector, addend: Vector) ->
    Vector
{
    return Vector(x: augend.x + addend.x,
        y: augend.y + addend.y, z: augend.z
        + addend.z)
}

var v1 = Vector(x:5, y:8, z:5)          {x 5, y 8, z 5}
var v2 = Vector(x:9, y:4, z:2)          {x 9, y 4, z 2}

//println(v1+v2)
```

Console Output

Figure 7-6: An operator overload allows us to add functionality to Swift operators.

Now that the addition operator has been instructed how to handle our "Vector" structures, add the following code to the example program in order to test the overload:

```
var v3 = v1 + v2
println("x:\(v3.x) y:\(v3.y) z:\(v3.z)")
```

The "v3" variable you've created is assigned the value of the sum of "v1" and "v2" and that addition is done according to the overload that we defined. When you print out each property from v3 you should see that they have been correctly calculated according to our "Vector" addition expression. Check your program output against figure 7-7.

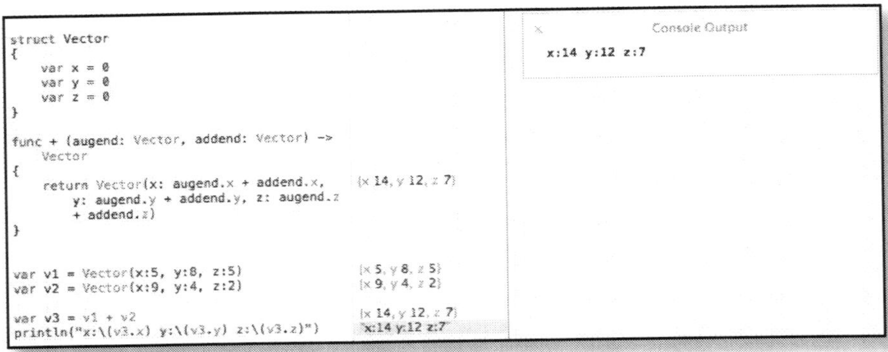

```
struct Vector
{
    var x = 0
    var y = 0
    var z = 0
}

func + (augend: Vector, addend: Vector) ->
    Vector
{
    return Vector(x: augend.x + addend.x,    {x 14, y 12, z 7}
        y: augend.y + addend.y, z: augend.z
        + addend.z)
}

var v1 = Vector(x:5, y:8, z:5)          {x 5, y 8, z 5}
var v2 = Vector(x:9, y:4, z:2)          {x 9, y 4, z 2}

var v3 = v1 + v2                        {x 14, y 12, z 7}
println("x:\(v3.x) y:\(v3.y) z:\(v3.z)")  x:14 y:12 z:7
```

Console Output

x:14 y:12 z:7

Figure 7-7: Once you've created an operator overload for the "Vector" structure, Swift is able to perform an addition operation on two vectors.

Operator overloads allow you increased flexibility when building your applications by allowing you to do more with standard operators. This makes structs, classes, enums and other custom types more versatile.

QUESTIONS FOR REVIEW

1. Operator overloading allows you to permanently modify the operators in Swift.
   a. True.
   b. False.

2. What is the correct syntax to overload an operator?
   a. func – (myVarA: Int, myVarB: Int) -> Int
   b. overload func – (myVarA: Int, myVarB: Int) -> Int
   c. func:overload – (myVarA: Int, myVarB: Int) -> Int
   d. func – (myVarA, myVarB) -> Int

3. Why are structures primarily used?
   a. To define abstract representations of objects.
   b. To contain a similar group of type-safe elements.
   c. To encapsulate a small set of simple values.
   d. As an alternative to classes.

4. Structures can contain properties and methods.
   a. True.
   b. False.

7.3 GENERICS

As we have been creating functions and methods we have been explicitly declaring the types of the arguments that we pass to them. One of the goals of efficient coding is to never repeat the same code, but sometimes when working with different data types, repetition seems inevitable. When you need a function to preform the same calculation on different data types, you're stuck creating multiple functions where the only difference is the name and definition syntax. A repetition problem such as this can be solved using **generics**.

Generics in Swift are functions that can work on any compatible data type. They allow you to avoid duplication and improve expressiveness in your code. Consider a situation where you want a function to test the equivalency of two arguments and return a Boolean. The code body of the function will be exactly the same, regardless of the data type you're testing. The only difference will be in the function declaration. Enter the following code in a new Xcode playground:

generics

```
func isEqualInt(a:Int, b:Int) -> Bool
{
    return a == b
}

println(isEqualInt(3,3)
println(isEqualInt(3.4,3.8)
```

The preceding code checks two Int values for equivalency. The two println() commands show the results of using the "isEqualInt()" function on an Int and then on a Double. Figure 7-8 shows the result:

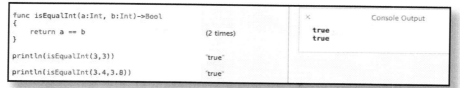

Figure 7-8: Our "isEqualInt()" function only works on Int values, but the code in the function's body would be identical for all data types.

The function returns the correct result for an Int, but an incorrect result for a Double. In order to get the same functionality for a Double, we would need to add the following code:

```
func isEqualDouble(a:Double, b:Double) ->
Bool
{
    return a == b
}

println(isEqualInt(3,3))
println(isEqualDouble(3.5,3.8))
```

After entering that code, your program should look like figure 7-9:

func isEqualInt(a:Int, b:Int)->Bool		Console Output
{		true
return a == b	true	false
}		
func isEqualDouble(a:Double, b:Double)->		
Bool		
{		
return a == b	false	
}		
println(isEqualInt(3,3))	"true"	
println(isEqualDouble(3.5,3.8))|	"false"	

Figure 7-9: Creating a new function for Doubles returns the proper value but it means that we have to write twice as much code.

As you can see, we now have the correct result for the case of a Double, but we had to create an entirely new function that largely consists of the same code. In order to get around the repetition problem we can use a generic function that will take any data type as an argument. Create a generic function using the following code:

```
func isEqual<T: Equatable>(a:T, b:T) ->
Bool
{
    return a == b
}

println(isEqual(3,3))
println(isEqual(3.3,3.5))
println(isEqual("3.3","3.3"))
println(isEqual(true,false))
```

In the preceding code we have followed the name of the function with a piece of code that instructs Swift to set "T" to the type of the arguments sent to the function if they are "Equatable." "Equatable" means that the arguments are all of the same type. The argument definition then declares that each argument will be of type "T." The remainder of the function is exactly the same as our previous examples. Figure 7-10 shows the results that you can expect.

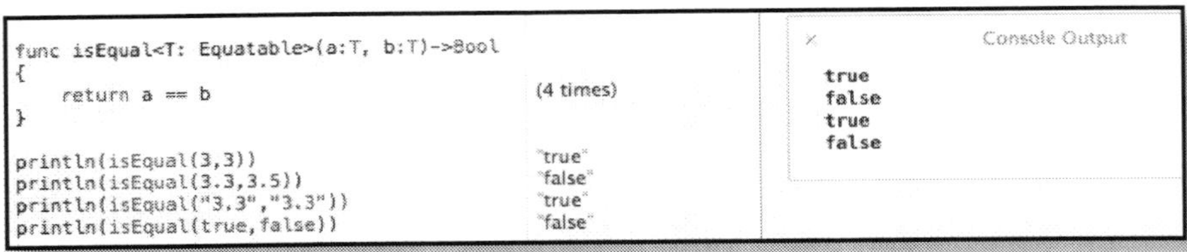

Figure 7-10: Generics can vastly reduce the amount of repeated code you have to write.

In the println() commands we have tested the function with Ints, Doubles, Strings, and Booleans. In all of those cases the function returns the correct results, saving us from rewriting the same code four times.

In the final section of this chapter we'll look at one of the more fun aspects of the Swift language, the use of emoji in your code.

QUESTIONS FOR REVIEW

1. Generics allow us to avoid code repetition.
   a. True.
   b. False.

2. What is the proper syntax to define a generic function?
   a. func myFunc (myVarA: T, myVarB: T)
   b. func myFunc:<T> (myVarA: T, myVarB: T)
   c. func myFunc<T: Equatable> (myVarA: T, myVarB: T)
   d. generic myFunc (myVarA, myVarB)

3. Generics are a good choice when we need to precisely know the type of the arguments in a function.
   a. True.
   b. False.

4. What is NOT an advantage of generics?
   a. Less code repetition.
   b. More readable and expressive code.
   c. Easier to debug.
   d. Add functionality to existing classes.

7.4 EMOJI

Emoji are small images intended to represent ideas or concepts. They were originally used in Japanese text messaging. The name comes from the Japanese "e," meaning picture, plus "moji," meaning character. Recently, hundreds of emoji have been incorporated into the Unicode standard for text encoding, allowing them to be used in a variety of places. In Swift, you can use emoji as names for your variables, classes, enums, structures, and other constructs.

Open a new Xcode playground and create a constant to store your name. Instead of using text to name the constant, though, use an emoji. To access the emoji menu in Swift, press control, command, and the space bar. You'll be presented with a menu, seen in figure 7-11, where you can select the emoji you want to use.

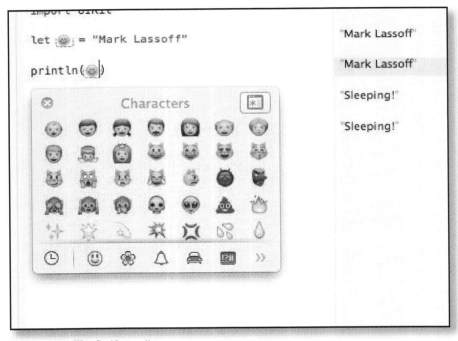

Figure 7-11: The Swift emoji menu.

Once you've chosen your emoji, Swift will consider it a completely valid constant name. In our example, we've chosen a smiley face to represent our name constant, and then instructed println() to print the value of the smiley face.

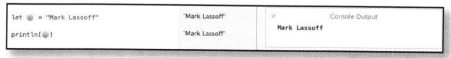

Figure 7-12: Swift will work with emojis as if they were any other element name.

You can also use multiple emoji to represent an element. In Figure 7-13, we've used three "zzz" emoji symbols to represent the string "Sleeping!"

Figure 7-13: Using multiple emoji characters to represent a variable.

Emoji are a neat little addition to Swift programming, but they might not be the most effective means of naming elements in your code. Still, they're a little bit of fun that you can have when you're developing your software in Swift.

1. "Emoji" comes from the Japanese "e" for picture plus "moji" for character.
   a. True.
   b. False.

2. What can you use emoji to replace? (Select all that apply)
   a. Variable names.
   b. Constant names.
   c. Class names.
   d. Structure names.

3. Extensive use of emoji would result in clear, easy to maintain and readable code.
   a. True.
   b. False.

4. What key combination do you use to access the emoji menu?
   a. control+alt+delete
   b. control+command+enter
   c. control+command+space
   d. control+command+alt

CHAPTER 7 LAB EXERCISE

1) Open a new playground called SLA_Lab7. In the text editor, erase any unnecessary code and leave the necessary import statement.

2) Create a multiline comment that lists your name, the date, and the name of the lab assignment (SLA_Lab7).

3) Enter the following code in a new Swift playground:

```
import UIKit

func feetToInchesInt(feet:Int) -> Double
{
    return Double(feet*12)
}

func feetToInchesDouble(feet:Double) ->
Double
{
    return feet*12
}

func feetToInchesFloat(feet:Float) -> Float
{
    return feet*12
}

func InchesToFeetInt(inches:Int) -> Double
{
    return Double(inches/12)
}

func InchestToFeetDouble(inches:Double) ->
Double
```

```
{
    return inches/12
}

func InchestToFeetFloat(inches:Double) ->
Double
{
    return inches/12
}

println(feetToInchesInt(177))
println(feetToInchesFloat(164.55))
println(InchesToFeetInt(1000))
```

4) Using what you learned about generics, encapsulate all of the methods listed into two generic methods. Change the function calls at the bottom of the code to use the generic methods that you created.

CHAPTER SUMMARY

In this chapter we have learned about additional useful features of the Swift programming language. We learned how extensions will allow us to increase the utility of built-in elements and classes. We explored using operator overloading to make operators more useful and thereby tailor them to our programs. We used generics to create functions that can handle any data type, thereby reducing our code repetition and allowing us to write cleaner, more transparent programs. Finally, we discovered that emoji can be used in Swift programming to add a little fun to our applications.

In the next and final chapter, we'll put all of our knowledge together and create an app!

CHAPTER 8

iOS 8 APP WITH SWIFT

CHAPTER OBJECTIVES:

- You will learn how to create an app layout in Xcode.
- You will utilize outlets and actions to link layout elements to code.
- You will learn how to use simulators to run a virtual iDevice.
- You will create and test an iPhone application using your knowledge of Swift and Xcode.

8.1 CREATING AN APP LAYOUT

Now that we have a solid understanding of the fundamentals of Swift programming, we're going to look at how Swift development connects to iOS in the Xcode IDE. To do this, we're going to create a simple program that will whet your appetite for further exploration of iOS development in Xcode with Swift.

Before we begin working on our sample program, we need to clearly define what it is that we want our program to accomplish. It is very important, as you continue on your programming adventures, that you specify and codify the goals of your programs before you begin development. In chapter one, we created a very basic iOS application that merely displayed the text "Hello World" on the screen. In our new program, we'll expand on that simple idea and create an app to greet the user. The app will ask for the user's name, take text input from the user, and then use that text input to display a welcome message personalized for the user. To keep it simple, we'll do all of these functions in a single view.

First, open Xcode. Instead of opening a playground, choose "Create a new Xcode project."

Welcome to Xcode

Version 6.0 (6A279r)

 Get started with a playground
Explore new ideas quickly and easily.

 Create a new Xcode project
Start building a new iPhone, iPad or Mac application.

 Check out an existing project
Start working on something from an SCM repository

Figure 8-1: Create a new project in Xcode instead of a playground.

Creating a new project brings up the template menu, shown in figure 8-2. The templates available allow us to quickly get started on various different types of projects. For our greetings app, we're going to select a Single View Application. The Single View Application is the simplest form of iOS app because it only features a single view to work with.

A **view** in iOS development is a rectangular area on the device screen that draws content, handles multitouch events, and manages the layout of any subviews. Every view created is an instance of the UIView class. We won't be creating any views in our example because the template implements a view that we will be modifying.

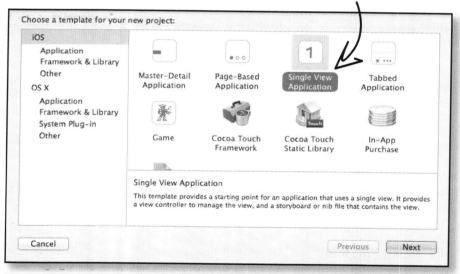

Figure 8-2: Xcode templates give you all of the basic files you need to begin creating a specific type of application.

Once you've selected your template, you have to name your program and choose a few basic options, as shown in figure 8-3. Recall the naming conventions we discussed in section 1.2. We'll follow those conventions here as well. For the "Product Name" we have chosen "HelloWorldiPhone," and for "Organization Name" we have chosen "LearnToProgram.tv." For the unique "Organization Identifier" we use the standard reverse URL format, "tv.learnToProgram" and append ".SwiftFundamentals" to further specify this project. If we released our app in the App Store, the identifier would be used by Apple to identify our application, so it's important that we make it unique. Finally, we choose Swift as our language preference and iPhone as our target device.

Choose options for your new project:

Product Name:	HelloWorldiPhone
Organization Name:	LearnToProgram.tv
Organization Identifier:	tv.learnToProgram.SwiftFundamentals
Bundle Identifier:	tv.learnToProgram.SwiftFundamentals.Hello...
Language:	Swift
Devices:	iPhone
	☐ Use Core Data

Cancel   Previous   Next

Figure 8-3: Project name and options.

Once the options are complete, Xcode will launch our new project. The project screen, shown in figure 8-4, presents us with the basic project information that we've just entered, as well as a number of additional project options. We explained some of these options in section 1.2 and we won't have to worry about them here. As you develop more complex programs, though, you will want to modify your project options.

Figure 8-4: The project screen. We're not going to modify our project settings at the moment.

When working in Xcode, the leftmost panel is called the "Navigator area," the center panel is called the "Editor area," and the rightmost panel is called the "Utility area." At the moment, you should have the "Project navigator" open in the Navigator area.

From the Project navigator in the Navigator area, select Main.storyboard. Selecting Main.storyboard will bring up your project's storyboard in the Editor area. Xcode has a convenient GUI to lay out project elements called the Interface Builder, seen in figure 8-5. In the Interface Builder you'll see a large arrow pointing to your view. That arrow is the initial scene indicator and it points to the view that is first loaded when the app is launched.

Figure 8-5: Your main storyboard, allowing you to lay out project elements.

In the bottom portion of the Utility area you'll see a set of icons, as shown in figure 8-6. This is the Object Library and it contains a set of objects that you can include in your program. Scroll through the list until you can see the "Label," "Button," and "Text Field" objects, as in figure 8-7.

Figure 8-6: The Object Library.

Tip: The Object Library gives you access to other included libraries by clicking on the icons across the top. They are, from left to right, the File Template Library, the Code Snippet Library, the Object Library, and the Media Library. If you can't see the objects shown in figure 8-6, you may be in the wrong library.

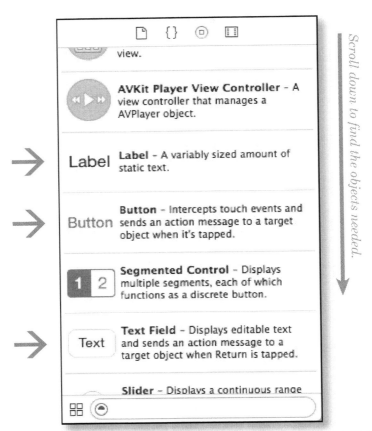

Figure 8-7: The objects that we're looking for in the Object Library are "Label," "Button," and "Text Field."

The first thing that we're going to do is display a title for our application. Our app greets users, so we can just call it "Greetings Application." The simplest way to create text is to click and drag the "Label" object from the Object library onto the view in the Interface Builder. As you click and drag the element around on the view, you'll notice blue dotted lines appearing. These lines are guides that will help you position and align elements. Align the application title on the top left corner of your view, as shown in figure 8-8.

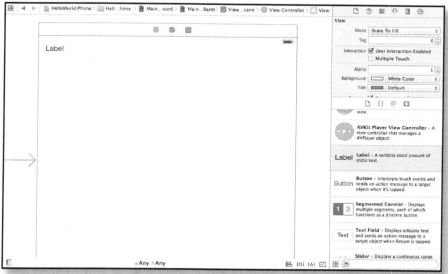

Figure 8-8: Align your label in the top left of your view.

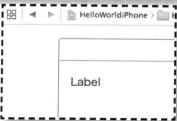

Once the label is in place, double click on it. You'll see that the label's text is highlighted and can be changed. Change the text so that it says "Greetings Application."

Once you're satisfied with the first label, use the same drag and drop technique to create a second label positioned below the first. The second label will be instructions that ask the user to enter their name, so change the text so that it reads "Enter Your Name."

Dragging and dropping objects doesn't just work for labels. In the Object Library, click and drag a "Text Field" object onto your view and position it between your two labels. The text field object is an empty text input box that a user can type string values into. In our sample application, the text field will be where your user inputs their name into the app. Some people have long names, so you may want to resize the text field after you've positioned it. To resize the text field, use the resize handles, which are the small white boxes on either side of the text field. Figure 8-9 shows you what your app should look like so far.

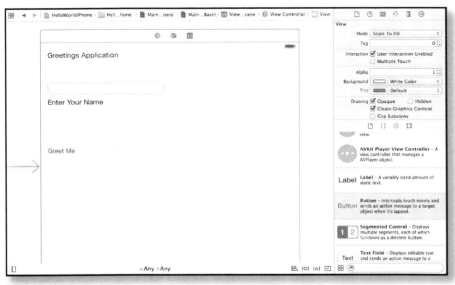

Figure 8-9: Your application with the directions and the text field added.

We now have a clear title, instructions, and a text input box. Our initial design also called for a personalized welcome message. Until now we have been sending output to a console window, but in an iOS app there is no console window. To display our output we will use a label that does not contain any text and then programmatically determine what it will display. Drag and drop another label onto your view, below the instructions.

Resize the label so that it can accommodate the string "Welcome" followed by a name, and then clear the default text data. When you clear the text data, you can either double click on the object in the view, as we have been doing, or use the label's Attributes inspector in the Utility area.

As seen in figure 8-10, above the Object Library is the Attributes inspector. The Attributes inspector has a selection of label attributes that can be changed, including the color, size, font, and alignment. At the moment, all that we're worried about is making sure that the Label Text field is empty. As you develop more complex programs you'll find the Attributes inspector very useful.

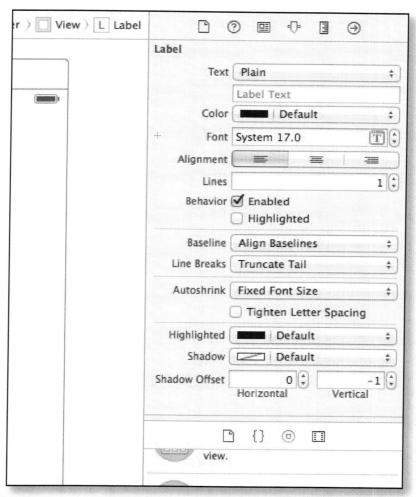

Figure 8-10: In the Utility area, above the Object Library, is the Attribute inspector.

> **Tip:** Like the Object Library panel, the Attribute inspector contains a number of other inspectors that can be chosen by clicking on the icons across the top. From left to right, they are the File inspector, the Quick Help inspector, the Identity inspector, the Attributes inspector, the Size inspector, and the Connections inspector.

We are almost done setting up the layout of our first app. The final piece of the puzzle is the button a user touches in order to display their personalized greeting. After adding labels and text fields you can probably guess how we add a button. Drag and drop the "Button" object from the Object Library into your view in the Interface Builder and place it below the empty label. Change the text of the button in the same manner that you changed the text of the labels so that it says "Greet Me." Your project should look like figure 8-11.

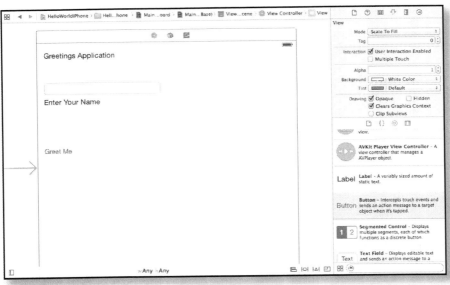

Figure 8-11: With the addition of a button, your project's layout is complete.

Our layout is complete, but our program won't do anything yet. The program code is not currently aware of the elements that we've created in the storyboard. Until we link those elements to our code using outlets and actions, we won't be able to do anything with what we have created. In the next section, we'll go over outlets and actions and create the code that will power our greetings app.

QUESTIONS FOR REVIEW

1. Which of the following is NOT an area in the Xcode project development window?
   a. Editor area.
   b. Utility area.
   c. Development area.
   d. Navigation area.

2. What is the purpose of a view?
   a. To draw content, handle multitouch events, and manage the layout of subviews.
   b. To display variable values.
   c. It serves the same purpose as the console output window in the playground.
   d. To determine which window is displayed in your app.

3. The Utility area contains the Object library and the Attributes inspector.
   a. True.
   b. False.

4. What is the name of the GUI used to create your app layout?
   a. Interface Creator.
   b. Layout Builder.
   c. Interface Builder.
   d. Interface Layout.

8.2 CREATING OUTLETS AND ACTIONS

After creating an app project and a layout in section 8.1, we have all of the elements that we need for our program to function as intended but we haven't built the code that powers it. In order to create that code, we will use **outlets** and **actions** to connect the elements that we've created to the code that will power our app.

outlets

Outlets allow objects in our code to reference an element that we've added to a storyboard. Actions map a method in our code and an element that we've created in our layout to an event. Xcode allows you to easily create these links in your Editor area.

actions

If it's not already open, open up your HelloWorldiPhone project in Xcode and load Main.storyboard into the Editor area. In order to create the outlet and action links from our layout elements to our code, we need to use the Assistant Editor. The icon to show the Assistant Editor is the fifth icon from the right on the unified toolbar at the top of the Xcode application window.

When the Assistant Editor is opened, it should be displaying ViewController.swift, as shown in figure 8-12. The ViewController.swift file is the Swift code that is associated with the view that we have been working on in Main.storyboard.

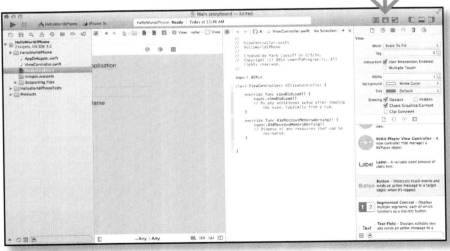

Figure 8-12: The Assistant Editor shows the code that powers the view we have been working on in the storyboard editor.

You can use the far right icon in the unified toolbar to toggle the display of the Utility area. We won't be using the Object library or the Attribute inspector anymore, so hide the Utility area to expand our active workspace. Figure 8-13 shows you how your Xcode environment should be laid out.

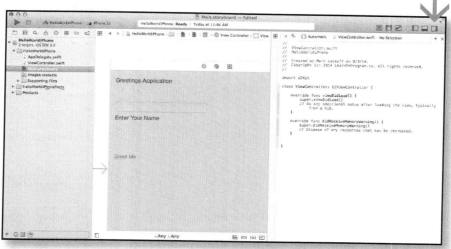

Figure 8-13: Hiding the Utility area gives us more room to work on our code.

You've probably noticed in the ViewController.swift file that there is a class, ViewController, which is a subclass of UIViewController. Within that class there are two override methods, "viewDidLoad()" and "didReceiveMemoryWarning()." The "viewDidLoad()" method determines what happens when the view loads and the "didReceiveMemoryWarning()" method determines what happens when the view receives an out of memory warning. By modifying these methods you can implement your own functionality, but we are not going to modify these methods right now. Instead, we are going to use our outlets and actions to link our storyboard elements to the ViewController class as properties and methods.

The technique to create an outlet or an action is control-dragging (hold the "control" key and then click and drag) an element from the view in the Interface Builder to the appropriate code location in the Assistant Editor.

In order to create an outlet, control-drag the text field from your layout into the body of the ViewController class. There will be a blue line extending from the text field element to the code editor and a solid horizontal blue bar in the code editor to show you where you will create the outlet. Once you've decided where to put the outlet, release the mouse button to drop it in place. A pop up will appear with options for the outlet you're about to create, as seen in figure 8-14.

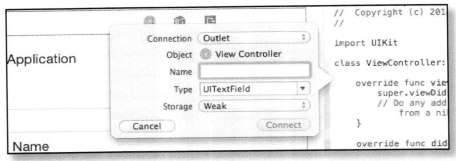

Figure 8-14: When creating an outlet in Xcode, this pop up displays the options available.

The "Connection" dropdown allows you to choose whether you want to create an outlet or an action. Select "outlet." The "Object" box tells you which object you have created a connection to. The "Name" text box is where you enter the name you want to refer to the layout object as. Enter "txtName" because we are connecting the user input text field. The "Type" dropdown allows you to pick the type of the element you're connecting. Finally, the "Storage" dropdown allows you to select whether you want the outlet to have a strong or weak reference. We will select "strong" for all of our outlets.

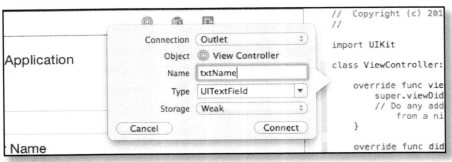

Figure 8-15: Name the outlet "txtName" because it refers to the input text box where a user enters their name.

Once you're ready, click "Connect" and your property will be created for you. You should see the following code in the ViewController class:

```
@IBOutlet var txtName: UITextField!
```

If the given code is not in the code body of the ViewController class, remove it and attempt to create the outlet again.

The previous code fragment is what creates the link between the view object that we have created in the Interface Builder, a UITextField, and the code that we want to use the view object in. The "@IBOutlet" keyword establishes that there is a connection between the layout and the code through an Interface Builder Outlet. After that, there is a variable declaration of "txtName" that is of type "UITextField." The exclamation mark after the variable type means that the variable is an implicitly unwrapped optional. An implicitly unwrapped optional is a variable that can be a nil value but is assumed to never actually be nil by the time it is used. At this point, it's not necessary to know exactly what an implicitly unwrapped optional is, it is enough just to know that it an implicitly unwrapped optional is required.

Figure 8-16 shows how your ViewController code should look in the Assistant Editor.

```
//
//  ViewController.swift
//  HelloWorldiPhone
//
//  Created by Mark Lassoff on 9/3/14.
//  Copyright (c) 2014 LearnToProgram.tv. All rights reserved.
//

import UIKit

class ViewController: UIViewController {

    @IBOutlet var txtName: UITextField!

    override func viewDidLoad() {
        super.viewDidLoad()
        // Do any additional setup after loading the view, typically
            from a nib.
    }

    override func didReceiveMemoryWarning() {
        super.didReceiveMemoryWarning()
        // Dispose of any resources that can be recreated.
    }

}
```

Figure 8-16: After creating the outlet for "txtName" your ViewController should look like this.

Use the same technique to create an outlet for the empty results label. Name it "lblResult" as shown in figure 8-17.

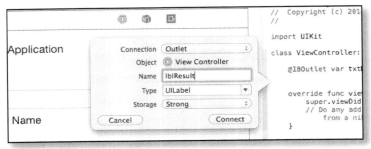

Figure 8-17: This outlet will link your code's output to the empty label you created in section 8.1.

The following code should have been inserted into your ViewController.

```
@IBOutlet var lblResult: UILabel!
```

Once that's complete, your complete ViewController should match figure 8-18.

```
⊞  ◀  ▶  🕙 Automatic  📄 ViewController.swift  Ⓒ ViewController        + ×

//
//  ViewController.swift
//  HelloWorldiPhone
//
//  Created by Mark Lassoff on 9/3/14.
//  Copyright (c) 2014 LearnToProgram.tv. All rights reserved.
//

import UIKit

class ViewController: UIViewController {

    @IBOutlet var txtName: UITextField!

    @IBOutlet var lblResult: UILabel!

    override func viewDidLoad() {
        super.viewDidLoad()
        // Do any additional setup after loading the view, typically
            from a nib.
    }

    override func didReceiveMemoryWarning() {
        super.didReceiveMemoryWarning()
        // Dispose of any resources that can be recreated.
    }
```

Figure 8-18: Both the input text field and the output label are connected to the ViewController code and are ready to be used.

The final connection step is to link the button in your layout to the ViewController code. Control-drag to create the link, as before, but set the connection to "Action" not "Outlet." A different set of options will be available, as you can see in figure 8-19.

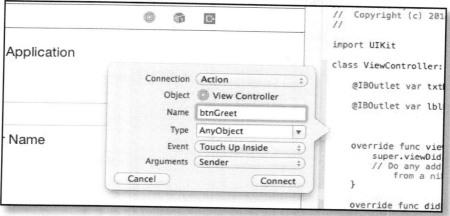

Figure 8-19: The options when creating an action link between your layout and your ViewController.

Set "Name" to "btnGreet", "Type" to "AnyObject," and "Arguments" to "Sender." If you select the "Event" option, you'll see a list of possible touch interactions and events that could cause the action to execute, shown in figure 8-20.

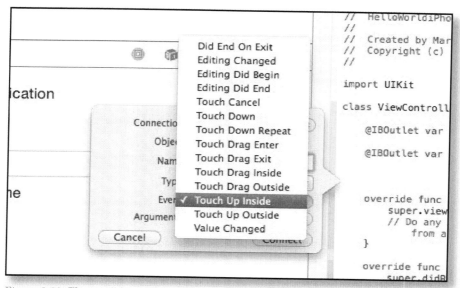

Figure 8-20: The possible events and interactions that could execute the action we are creating.

We want "Greet Me" to be a standard button that executes when a user touches it, so select "Touch Up Inside." You'll see that an empty method has appeared inside your ViewController class, like in figure 8-21.

```swift
//
//  ViewController.swift
//  HelloWorldiPhone
//
//  Created by Mark Lassoff on 9/3/14.
//  Copyright (c) 2014 LearnToProgram.tv. All rights reserved.
//

import UIKit

class ViewController: UIViewController {

    @IBOutlet var txtName: UITextField!

    @IBOutlet var lblResult: UILabel!


    @IBAction func btnGreet(sender: AnyObject) {
    }

    override func viewDidLoad() {
        super.viewDidLoad()
        // Do any additional setup after loading the view, typically
            from a nib.
    }

    override func didReceiveMemoryWarning() {
        super.didReceiveMemoryWarning()
        // Dispose of any resources that can be recreated.
    }

}
```

Figure 8-21: The ViewController class after linking the "Greet Me" button to it with an action.

The empty method we just created is where you'll put the code that you want to execute when the "Greet Me" button is touched. You can see that the method is given the name "btnGreet()." In the "btnGreet()" method enter the following code:

```swift
var theName:String = txtName.text
lblResult.text = "Welcome \(theName)"
```

In the method we are declaring a variable named "theName" that is explicitly typed as a String, and we are assigning to it the value of the "text" property of our "txtName" UITextField object. The "text" property holds the data that the user input into the text box in our layout. We are then setting the value of the "text" property of our "lblResult" UILabel object to "Welcome \(theName)." The "text" property of a UILable object is the text data that is displayed by the label. By doing this, we are using the input from the user to personalize the greeting that our app returns. Figure 8-22 shows you what your complete ViewController should look like.

```swift
//
//  ViewController.swift
//  HelloWorldiPhone
//
//  Created by Mark Lassoff on 9/3/14.
//  Copyright (c) 2014 LearnToProgram.tv. All rights reserved.
//

import UIKit

class ViewController: UIViewController {

    @IBOutlet var txtName: UITextField!

    @IBOutlet var lblResult: UILabel!


    @IBAction func btnGreet(sender: AnyObject) {
        var theName:String = txtName.text
        lblResult.text = "Welcome \(theName)"
    }

    override func viewDidLoad() {
        super.viewDidLoad()
        // Do any additional setup after loading the view, typically
            from a nib.
    }

    override func didReceiveMemoryWarning() {
        super.didReceiveMemoryWarning()
        // Dispose of any resources that can be recreated.
    }

}
```

Figure 8-22: The complete ViewController class.

We now have completed the code for the simple app that we designed in section 8.1. In order to test it we will use a feature of Xcode that simulates iOS devices.

1. What technique creates an outlet or action?
   a. Shift-click and drag an element from the layout to the code.
   b. Control-click and drag an element from the layout to the code.
   c. Control-click an element and then click on the desired location in code.
   d. Click and drag an element from the layout to the code.

2. What will creating an outlet do?
   a. Insert the appropriately named variable into your code.
   b. Insert an unnamed variable into your code.
   c. Insert the appropriately named method into your code.
   d. Insert an unnamed method into your code.

3. What is required in order to create an action?
   a. Nothing, it is complete upon being created.
   b. An override of the parent classes implementation of viewDidLoad().
   c. Code to complete a named method shell.
   d. Code to complete an unnamed method shell.

4. Creating an action allows you to choose the touch event that causes the action to execute.
   a. True.
   b. False.

8.3 RUNNING AND TESTING YOUR APP

We now have a basic yet fully functioning iOS application that we need to test. Xcode has a means of testing your applications without having to install them on an actual device. We briefly introduced Xcode simulations in section 1.2, and in this section we will again use those simulations to test our app.

First, open your HelloWorldiPhone application project in Xcode. Once everything is running, create an iOS device simulator. In the Xcode menu, select "Open Developer Tool" and then "iOS Simulator," as shown in figure 8-23.

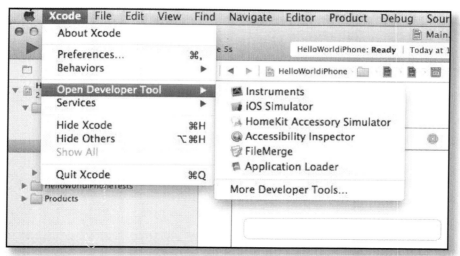

Figure 8-23: In order to create an iOS Simulator, choose the "Open Developer Tool" menu from the "Xcode" menu.

When you create a simulator, you are creating a virtual version of a physical device using software on your Mac. Creating a virtual device in software can be very hardware intensive, so expect the simulator to take some time to load when you first run it.

Once your simulator is running, return to your Xcode project. In the upper left-hand corner of the Xcode window there is a "Run" arrow button, as seen in figure 8-24. When you click on the button your application will build. This process takes your code and compiles it into a format that can run on an iDevice. Compiling can be a lengthy process, so be prepared to wait for a few minutes.

Figure 8-24: The "Run" button in the upper left-hand corner will build your application.

When the application finishes building it will launch in the simulator you've just started. You should see your iPhone app running, like in figure 8-25.

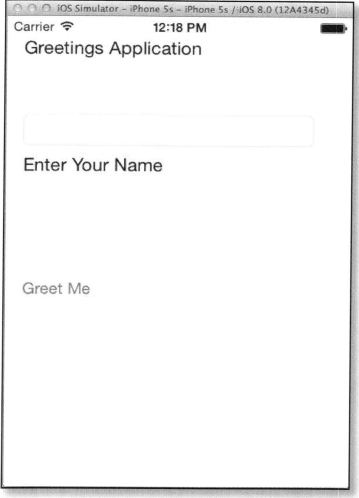

Figure 8-25: Your app running in an iPhone 5s simulator. The title bar gives you information about the type of device you're simulating and the iOS version.

You can interact with your simulator using your mouse to emulate touching the screen. Click on the text box we created for a user to enter their names.

Figure 8-26: The simulator registers your mouse clicks as touch events.

After you click on the text box, the iPhone's on-screen keyboard will pop up, as shown in figure 8-26. You can use the on-screen keyboard to enter your name, or you can type it in using your computer keyboard.

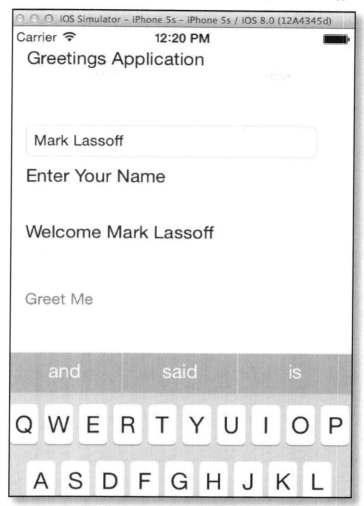

Figure 8-27: After you've entered your name and clicked "Greet Me" your program displays its greeting!

With your name input into the text box, click the "Greet Me" button we created. You should see the output shown in figure 8-27. Recall that we linked that button to a method in the ViewController class. When our app runs, a ViewController object is instantiated, allowing us to execute the "btnGreet()" method. The "btnGreet()" method then modifies the "text" property of "lblResult" to show our greeting. Congratulations, your app works!

You've tested your application on a simulated iPhone, but if you were developing an app you planned on releasing you would probably want to test it on multiple devices. You can do this in Xcode by changing the simulated device. With your Xcode project selected, look to the right of the "Run" button. You'll see the name of your application and then the device you currently have selected as the build target. Click on that device to access a menu, which allows you to change the target. Figure 8-28 illustrates the simulator device selection.

Figure 8-28: You can change the device that you're simulating.

Once you have a new device selected, rebuild your application. To rebuild the app, press the square "Stop" button that's next to the "Run" button. This will stop the current simulation. Press "Run" again to restart the new simulation with a different device. In figure 8-29 you can see the same app running on a simulated iPad Air.

Using simulators it's possible to test your application on a variety of different iDevices to ensure compatibility.

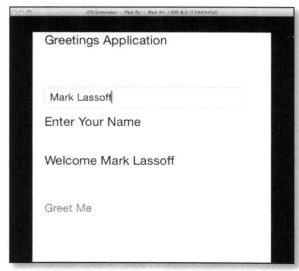

Figure 8-29: Our Greeting app running in a simulated iPad Air.

QUESTIONS FOR REVIEW

1. What is the purpose of simulators in Xcode?
   a. To simulate user interaction.
   b. To simulate an app store page.
   c. To simulate a physical device for testing purposes.
   d. To display console output from an app.

2. Xcode can simulate different iPhones and iPads.
   a. True.
   b. False.

3. A physical device is required to be connected to your computer to run a simulator.
   a. True.
   b. False.

4. What does the "Run" button in Xcode do?
   a. It builds your program and outputs an executable file.
   b. It builds your program and runs it on a simulator.
   c. It is the only way to create a simulator.
   d. It builds your program and runs it on OS X.

CHAPTER 8 LAB EXERCISE

1) Create a new Project. Instead of a playground, choose File -> New and Project from the dropdown menus.

2) Choose a Single View Application from the menu and click Next.

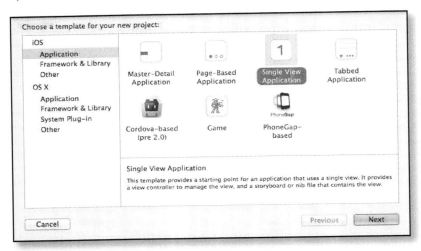

3) Fill out the next screen of the wizard as shown. You may change the value of Organization and Organization identifier fields to reflect your own name or company.

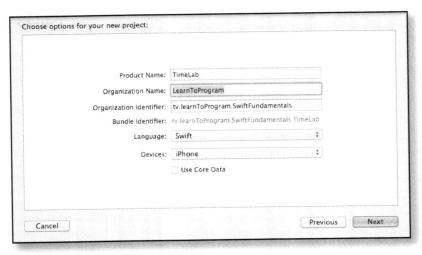

4) At the next screen, save the project where you'd like.

5) From the menu on the right side of XCode, choose Main.storyboard so that you may design the interface.

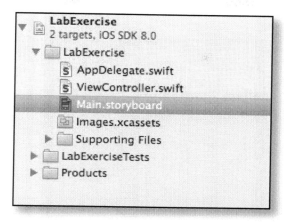

6) Using the Label, Button, and Text Field controls, design an interface that looks similar to this example:

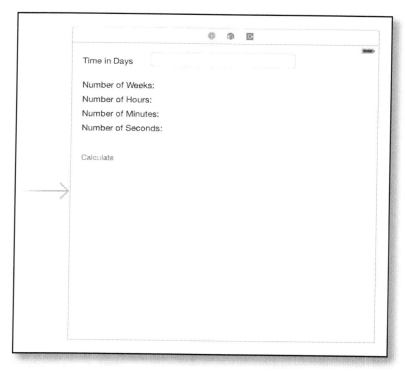

7) To the right of the Number of Weeks, Number of Hours, Number of Minutes, and Number of Seconds labels, create an additional blank label that will hold a value. Make sure the new labels are wide enough to accommodate a wide label. With all your blank labels selected, your interface should look something like this:

8) Click the "Show Assistant Editor" button towards the upper right of XCode. This will open the assistant editor with the code for the view you are creating.

Your screen should look similar to this:

9) Hold the CTRL key and drag from the label to the right of the "Number of Weeks:" text to just below the line of code that begins "class ViewController."

10) In the outlet pop-up that appears, fill out the name lblWeeks. You can leave the rest of the default items.

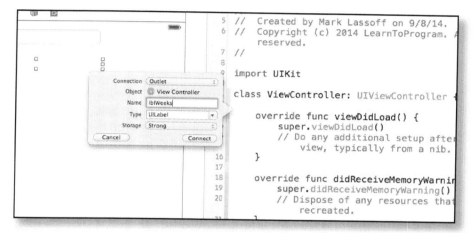

11) Create the rest of the necessary actions and outlets for the program. Don't forget the text field at the top where the user will input the "Time in Days," and the button at the bottom.

12) Create the necessary Swift code so that when the program runs and the user types in a time in days and clicks the button, the values for weeks, hours, minutes, and seconds are displayed. Use appropriate variable types to provide the most accurate results possible.

CHAPTER SUMMARY

Congratulations, you've made your first iPhone app! You now have a basic idea of how Swift connects with the iPhone through the Xcode IDE and you've learned the basics of programming in the Swift programming language. You've also learned the most important foundational concepts in computer programming: variables, constants, conditionals, functions, classes, and object-oriented programming. From here, you'll be able to learn about more advanced programming concepts and how those concepts apply to the Swift language.

Swift, an expressive, powerful and versatile new programming language, is the way to create new and exciting apps for iPhones, iPads, and other Apple products. Apple has said that they intend Swift to be the premier programming language for their products. Your knowledge of Swift programming allows you to get in on the ground floor of this exciting new paradigm in iOS development and we encourage you to continue your exploration of the vast and rewarding world of programming. Good luck!

ANSWER KEY

Chapter 1

Section 1.1
1. What does IDE stand for?
   b. Integrated Development Environment

2. What does the gutter allow us to do?
   b. Keep track of our variable values.

3. How do you define an Int variable in Swift?
   c. Declare the variable and assign a value:
   var a = 5

4. Which of the following is NOT a Swift variable type?
   c. Long.

Section 1.2
1. What is a good use for comments in code?
   b. To clearly and concisely document your code for future reference.

2. What do Swift templates provide? Choose all that apply.
   b. The basic files that you need for a certain project type to work.
   d. An outline for you to work within in order to speed up development.

3. Why is it standard to use a reverse URL when creating an Organization Identifier?
   d. To help ensure that they're unique.

4. What does Xcode do when you run an iPhone app that you're developing?
   a. Launch an iPhone emulator to run your app.

Chapter 2

Section 2.1
1. What is "Camel Case?"
   b. A naming convention that capitalizes the first letter of each word.

2. How can variables be typed?
   c. Implicit or explicit.

3. What can you NOT do to a constant?
   d. Modify its value.

4. What should you consider when naming variables? Choose all that apply.
   a. How long the variable name is.
   b. How readable the variable name is.
   c. How relevant the variable name is.
   d. How clearly the name expresses what the variable is meant to represent.

Section 2.2
1. Which of the following are types of the Int variable type? Choose all that apply.
   a. Int8.
   b. Int16.
   d. Int64.

2. A Float is more precise than a Double.
   b. False.

3. The answer to question 2 can only be either true or false. Which variable type would best be able to hold that value?
   c. Boolean.

4. Why will Swift assign a Double instead of a Float when implicitly typing a variable?
   a. Swift is choosing the safer option because it does not know how precise you will need your variable to be.

Section 2.3
1. Which of the following is NOT an example of an arithmetic operator used in Swift?
   c. #

2. What is the purpose of the "%" operator?
   b. It returns the remainder from a division operation between the two values.

3. What is a use of the modulus operator?
   a. Finding out if a number is even.

4. The right side of an assignment operation is evaluated first.
   a. True.

Section 2.4
1. What does typecasting do?
   c. It uses the value of a variable but casts it as a specified type.

2. A Double converted to an Int will be rounded appropriately.
   b. False.

3. Variable type declarations are permanent.
   a. True.

4. What is proper syntax for typecasting?
   a. floatValue = (Double)intValue

Section 2.5
1. What is String interpolation?
   b. Including variables, constants, literals, or expressions in a String literal.

2. What is the proper method of String concatenation in Swift?
   b. stringA + stringB

3. String interpolation does not work with expressions.
   b. False.

4. Can typecasting be a part of string interpolation?
   a. Yes.

Chapter 3

Section 3.1
1. What is the purpose of flow control?
   a. It determines what code is run at what time.

2. Which of the following is not a comparison operator?
   c. =

3. An else-statement runs whether or not the preceding if-statement ran.
   b. False.

4. How does an if-statement know if it should run?
   c. It only runs if its statement evaluates to "true."

Section 3.2

1. Which of the following symbols is used to represent "and?"
   d. &&

2. In the following statement:

   a > b || a > c

   which of the following cases would return true?
   c. a = 2, b = 1, c = 2 ·

3. When is the final else-statement executed in a complex conditional?
   b. When all of the previous if-statements are false.

4. Only one if-statement in an if-else block of code will be run.
   a. True.

Section 3.3

1. Does every case in a switch statement require curly brackets?
   b. No.

2. When does the default case run in a switch statement?
   b. It will only run when no other cases are true.

3. Switch statements do not evaluate if a String is uppercase or lowercase when evaluating their value.
   b. False.

4. Is a default block required in a switch statement?
   a. Yes.

Section 3.4

1. How is a while-loop initialized?
   b. Using the "while" keyword and a conditional statement.

2. Which of the following is a good situation to use a loop?
   c. When you need to iterate through a set of data.

3. In a while-loop, the condition is tested before the code runs for the first time.
   a. True.

4. Counters used in loops can only count incrementally.
   b. False.

Section 3.5

1. Are a for-loop and a while-loop interchangeable?
   a. Yes.

2. A for-loop requires its test value to be incremented in the body of the loop.
   b. False.

3. Which of the following is not a part of the for-loop construct?
   c. Condiment.

4. Can an expression be used when declaring the test value or condition of a for-loop?
   a. Yes.

Section 3.6

1. Which of the following statements is true?
   c. For-in-loops use a named constant when iterating through Array elements.

2. You must explicitly state how many iterations you want a for-in-loop to go through.
   b. False.

3. What is the difference between an open range operator and a half-closed range operator?
   b. A half-closed range operator does not iterate through the end value while an open range operator does.

4. What is the proper syntax for a half-closed range operator?
   b. 1..<9

Chapter 4

Section 4.1

1. What is the difference between a mutable and immutable array?
   c. An immutable array cannot be modified but a mutable array can.

2. Which of the following is NOT a correct array declaration?
   d. var myArray = (1.0,2.0,3.0)

3. An array can contain different variable types.
   b. False.

4. In order to access an array member, what do we need to know?
   a. index.

Section 4.2
1. Why is it important to be able to use Array.Count() to get the length of an array?
   b. Because we won't always know the exact length of the arrays we'll be working with.

2. Given an array named "myArray," which of the following is the proper syntax for Array.Count()?
   d. myArray.count

3. What does Array.Slice() allow us to do?
   a. Return a subset of an array.

4. Given an array named "myArray" and two integer values "a" and "b," which of the following is the proper syntax for Array.Slice()?
   c. myArray[a...b]

Section 4.3
1. What is the proper usage of Arrays.append()?
   c. Arrays.append() is used to add a member to the end of an array.

2. If Arrays.Insert() is called without the "atIndex:" keyword, the function automatically inserts a member at the end of the array.
   b. False.

3. What syntax would you use to concatenate myArrayA and myArrayB?
   a. myArrayA += myArrayB

4. Attempting to use Array.RemoveLast() on an empty array will return an error.
   a. True.

Section 4.4
1. What data type is a dictionary?
   c. Collection.

2. What is the correct syntax to explicitly declare a dictionary?
   d. var myDictionary:[Int:String] = [1:"value", 2:"value2"]

3. Dictionaries use an index as well as a key-value pair.
   b. False.

4. How do you access the members of a dictionary in a for-in loop?
   a. for (key, value) in myDictionary

Section 4.5
1. What syntax would correctly add a new member to the dictionary "myDictionary?"
   c. myDictionary[4321] = "Jones"

2. Modifying a dictionary member using the assignment operator is a valid technique.
   a. True.

3. What does Dictionary.UpdateValue() do?
   c. It updates the value of a dictionary member and returns the original value.

4. Which are NOT ways to remove a member from a dictionary? Choose all that apply.
   b. myDictionary.delete(1234)
   d. myDictionary -= myDictionary[1234]

Chapter 5

Section 5.1
1. Functions allow us to reuse blocks of code.
   a. True.

2. In order to create a function called "myFunction," what syntax would you use?
   c. func myFunction()

3. Where does a function need to be declared in order for it to be used in a program?
   c. A function may be declared anywhere in the code.

4. When is the code within a function executed?
   a. Function code is executed only when the function is called.

Section 5.2
1. What is the purpose of arguments?
   a. Arguments allow us to pass information to functions to be processed.

2. Which of the following is a proper function declaration?
   c. func myFunction(arg1:Int, arg2:String)

3. Functions can take more than one argument.
   a. True.

4. Xcode's code completion bubbles will ignore our functions.
   b. False.

Section 5.3
1. Why is it useful to return values from functions?
   a. In order to use the function's resulting data in our program.

2. A function can take parameters and also return a value.
   a. True.

3. We cannot assign the returned value from a function to a variable.
   b. False.

4. What is the correct syntax for a function that returns a value?
   c. func myFunction()->String

Section 5.4
1. In programming, scope refers to the visibility of a variable to other parts of the program.
   a. True.

2. How would you declare a variable with global scope?
   c. It would be declared outside of any functions.

3. Which is true of a local variable?
   a. It can be used within the function that it is declared.

4. Function arguments are local.
   a. True.

Section 5.5
1. A nested function can be called from anywhere in the program.
   b. False.

2. What do nested functions allow us to do? (Choose all that apply)
   a. Better organize our code.
   b. Limit repeated code in our program.
   d. Encapsulate code blocks within a function.

3. Code indentation is not considered by the Swift compiler.
   a. True.

4. Xcode's code completion bubble ignores nested functions.
    b. False.

Chapter 6

Section 6.1
1. Using enumeration is a type safe way to work with groups of similar data.
    a. True.

2. What is a proper enum declaration?
    a. enum myEnum { // member definition }

3. What happens when you assign a variable of type enum the value of an undeclared member?
    c. Xcode produces a type error.

4. Which of the following would be a good candidate for enumeration?
    d. All of the above.

Section 6.2
1. What do classes allow you to do in your program?
    b. Create abstract representations of real-world objects.

2. Which of the following is a proper class declaration?
    c. class myClass { // class code block }

3. What does init() do within a class?
    a. Initializes properties when the class is instantiated.

4. Functions that are declared within classes are known as "methods."
    a. True.

Section 6.3
1. It is often useful to have subclasses that are completely unrelated to their parent class.
    b. False.

2. What is the proper syntax to define a subclass?
    c. class mySubclass:myClass { // subclass code block }

3. An override allows a subclass to implement a different version of its parent class' method.
    a. True.

4. What is one benefit of object-oriented programming?
   a. Better organization and structure in large programs.

Section 6.4
1. Does a protocol definition require method implementation?
   b. No.

2. Protocols have to be implemented with classes within the same hierarchy.
   b. False.

3. How does Xcode react to a class with a protocol implemented that does not yet have its requirements met?
   b. Xcode will generate an error.

4. Protocols determine the specifics of how their requirements are implemented in a given class.
   b. False.

Chapter 7

Section 7.1
1. What is an extension?
   a. A means of adding functionality to existing code elements.

2. What is the proper syntax for an extension?
   b. extension Double

3. An extension will modify the original code for the element it's extending.
   b. False.

4. What does a computed property allows us to do?
   c. Assign a value according to the evaluation of a code block.

Section 7.2
1. Operator overloading allows you to permanently modify the operators in Swift.
   b. False.

2. What is the correct syntax to overload an operator?
   a. func – (myVarA: Int, myVarB: Int)-> Int

3. Why are structures primarily used?
   c. To encapsulate a small set of simple values.

4. Structures can contain properties and methods.
   a. True.

Section 7.3
1. Generics allow us to avoid code repetition.
   a. True.

2. What is the proper syntax to define a generic function?
   c. func myFunc<T: Equatable> (myVarA: T, myVarB: T)

3. Generics are a good choice when we need to precisely know the type of the arguments in a function.
   b. False.

4. What is NOT an advantage of generics?
   d. Add functionality to existing classes.

Section 7.4
1. "Emoji" comes from the Japanese "e" for picture plus "moji" for character.
   a. True.

2. We can use emoji to replace (Select all that apply)
   a. Variable names.
   b. Constant names.
   c. Class names.
   d. Structure names.

3. Extensive use of emoji would result in clear, easy to maintain and readable code.
   b. False.

4. What key combination do you use to access the emoji menu?
   c. control+command+space

Chapter 8

Section 8.1
1. Which of the following is NOT an area in the Xcode project development window?
   c. Development area.

2. What is the purpose of a view?
   a. To draw content, handle multitouch events and manage the layout of subviews.

3. The Utility area contains the Object library and the Attributes inspector.
   a. True.

4. What is the name of the GUI used to create your app layout?
   c. Interface Builder.

Section 8.2
1. What technique creates an outlet or action?
   b. Control-click and drag an element from the layout to the code.

2. What will creating an outlet do?
   a. Insert the appropriately named variable into your code.

3. What is required in order to create an action?
   c. Code to complete a named method shell.

4. Creating an action allows you to choose the touch event that causes the action to execute.
   a. True.

Section 8.3
1. What is the purpose of simulators in Xcode?
   c. To simulate a physical device for testing purposes.

2. Xcode can simulate different iPhones and iPads.
   a. True.

3. A physical device is required to be connected to your computer to run a simulator.
   b. False.

4. What does the "Run" button in Xcode do?
   b. It builds your program and runs it on a simulator.

Appendix

Action	In iOS, an action is a link between a method in code and an element in the Interface Builder.
Arguments	Arguments are input values passed to a function to match the function's parameters.
Arithmetic Operators	Arithmetic operators are operators that perform standard mathematical functions. Swift supports addition (+), subtraction (-), multiplication, (*) and division (/).
Arrays	An array is a collection type that stores a set of values of the same type in a zero-indexed list.
Assignment Operator	The assignment operator (=) is used to initialize or update the value of an element.
Boolean	Boolean values are logical values that can only ever be true or false.
Camel Case	Camel case is a standard naming convention in which an element is given a clear, multi-word name that is written as a single word that begins with a lowercase letter and in which the first letter of every contained word is uppercase.
Character	A character is a single Unicode-compliant symbol.
Class	A class is a general purpose construct used to create abstract representation of real-world objects and concepts. Classes are the building blocks of modern programs.
class	"class" is the keyword used to create a class in Swift.
Collection Type	Collection types are data types that are intended to store collections of values.
Comments	Comments are non-executable blocks of text in the code that are intended as a description, note, or reminder.

Comparison Operators	Comparison operators are logical operators that test conditions. They are: equal to (==), not equal to (!=), greater than (>), less than (<), greater than or equal to (>=), and less than or equal to (<=).
Complex Conditionals	Complex conditionals are conditional statements with multiple if-statements in their code block.
Compound Conditionals	Compound conditionals are conditional statements that have more than one condition, separated by the logical and (&&) or or (| |) statements.
Computed Properties	Computed properties are properties of a class or structure that are calculated rather than stored.
Concatenation	Concatenation is the operation of joining Strings and arrays together.
Constant	A constant is a value that is stored in memory and referred to by its name. Constants are immutable, meaning that they cannot be changed.
Control Flow	Control flow is the use of conditional statements to determine the flow of execution of code.
Decrement	To decrement is to decrease the value of a variable by a value.
Dictionary	A dictionary is a collection type that stores a set of values of the same type according to key-value pairs.
Double	Doubles are numbers with a fractional component. Doubles represent a 64-bit floating point number. Doubles are more precise than Floats.
Emoji	Emoji are picture characters that originated in Japan.
enum	"enum" is the keyword used to declare an enumeration in Swift.
Enumerations	Enumerations are a defined common type for a group of related values that enables those values to be used in a type safe way.

Explicit Type	An explicit type is a variable or constant that has its type chosen by the programmer.
extension	"extension" is the keyword used to define an extension in Swift.
Extensions	Extensions are new functionality added to structures, classes, and enumeration types.
Float	Floats are numbers with a fractional component. Floats represent a 32-bit floating point number. Floats are not as precise as Doubles.
For-in-Loop	A for-in-loop is a loop type intended to iterate over collections, including members of an array, characters in a String, and ranges of numbers.
For-Loop	A for-loop is a loop type that includes an initialization, condition, and incrementer.
func	"func" is the keyword used to create a function in Swift.
Function	A function is a named, self-contained code block that performs a specific task.
Function Call	A function call is the method of executing the code block contained in a function by referring to the function's name and passing any required arguments.
Generics	Generics are functions and types written to utilize any data type. Generics are used to avoid unnecessary code duplication.
Global	A globally scoped element is visible and can be accessed from anywhere in the program.
If-Else Statement	An if-else statement is a conditional block where the if conditional executes if its condition is true and the else condition executes otherwise.
If-Statement	An if-statement is a conditional that executes if its condition is true.
Implicit Type	An implicit type is a variable or constant that has its type inferred by Swift.
Increment	To increment is to increase the value of a variable by a value.

init	"init" is the keyword for a function's initializer method.
Initializer	An initializer is a special method in a class that is executed when the class is instantiated and usually sets class properties.
Instance	An instance is an instantiated example of a class that can be assigned properties and used in code.
Instantiate	To instantiate is to create an instance of a class that can be assigned properties and used in code.
Int	An Int is a whole number with no fractional component. Ints can be different sizes: Int8, Int16, Int32 and Int64. In Swift, "Int" refers to "Int32" on a 32-bit platform and "Int64" on a 64-bit platform.
Integrated Development Environment (IDE)	An Integrated development environment, or IDE, is a software application that provides a set of tools for programmers to use when they're developing software.
let	"let" is the keyword used to declare constants.
Local	A locally scoped element is visible and can be accessed only within the element that created it.
Loop	A loop is a control flow statement that executes a code block multiple times if its condition is true.
Method	A method is a code block within a class that provides functionality to that class and is declared in a similar manner to a function.
Nested Functions	Nested functions are functions that are created within other functions, scoping them locally to their parent function.
Object	An object is an instantiated example of a class that can be assigned properties and used in code.

Object Oriented Programming (OOP)	Object-oriented programming, or OOP, is the technique of architecting programs using classes and instantiated objects as building blocks.
Operator Overloading	Object overloading is a technique to add new functionality to existing operators.
Outlet	In iOS, an outlet is a link between a code object and an Interface Builder element.
override	"override" is the keyword that defines a subclass method which modifies the implementation of a similarly named parent class method.
Parameters	Parameters are values that a function expects to be passed as arguments in order to execute its code block.
Postfix Operator	A postfix operator evaluates an increment or decrement after the evaluation of an expression.
Prefix Operator	A prefix operator evaluates an increment or decrement before the evaluation of an expression.
Properties	Properties are values stored within a class.
protocol	"protocol" is the keyword used to define a protocol.
Protocol	A protocol is the blueprint of methods and properties used to enforce a task on a class, structure or enumeration. No implementation is defined in a protocol.
Range Operator	A range operator is a shortcut for expressing ranges of values.
Return Value	A return value is the result of a code block that is returned so it can be stored or processed further.
Scope	Scope is the visibility of elements in a program.
Simulator	A simulator is a virtual version of a physical iDevice for testing purposes in Xcode.
String	A String is a collection of characters.

String Interpolation	String interpolation is the construction of a new String literal from a mix of variables, expressions, constants, and literals.
struct	"struct" is the keyword to define a structure.
Structure	A structure is a general-purpose construct used to create abstract representation of real world objects and concepts, but is generally used in place of a class when its purpose is to encapsulate a small amount of basic data values.
Subclasses	Subclasses are classes that inherit the properties and methods of a parent class in a hierarchical manner.
Switch Statement	A switch statement is a control flow statement that tests a condition against a set of possible cases and executes only the code block of the true case, or a default case if no other cases are true. Swift requires switch statements to be exhaustive.
Type Safety	Type safety is a programming language feature that enforces type checks in order to ensure that the correct types of values are being used.
Typecasting	Typecasting is a technique to use the value of a variable as if it were a specific type.
var	"var" is the keyword used to declare variables.
Variable	A variable is a value that is stored in memory and referred to by its name. Variables can be changed.
View	In iOS programming, a View is a class that manages a rectangular section of the screen and is responsible for drawing content, handling multitouch events, and managing the layout of subviews.
While-Loop	A while-loop is a loop type that continues to execute as long as its condition is true.

The Development Club

https://learntoprogram.tv/course/ultimate-monthly-bundle/?coupon=BOOK19

This comprehensive membership includes:

• Access to EVERY course in LearnToProgram's growing library--including our exciting lineup of new courses planned for the coming year. This alone is over a $3,000 value.

• Access to our Live Courses. Take any of our online instructor-led courses which normally cost up to $300. These courses will help you advance your professional skills and learn important techniques in web, mobile, and game development.

• Free certification exams. As you complete your courses, earn LearnToProgram's certifications by passing optional exams. All certification fees are waived for club members.

• Weekly instructor hangouts where you can ask questions about course material, your personal learning goals, or just chat!

• Free Personal Learning Plans. You'll never wonder what you should take next to achieve your goals!

• The LearnToProgram guarantee!

THE LEARNTOPROGRAM GUARANTEE

Our Guarantee:
If you watch the course videos and complete the lab exercises, **you will learn to program.** Guaranteed. If you don't, we will personally pay your membership fees for the next 90 days.

The Development Club

Use Coupon Code: BOOK19
and get $20 off your first month!

More Information at
https://LearnToProgram.tv

Made in the USA
Lexington, KY
13 October 2014